A Boy's Life
in the Baby Boom

True Tales from Small Town America

BY JAMES HERBERT SMITH

For Trish

Enjoy!

James Herbert Smith

ALSO BY JAMES HERBERT SMITH

- A Passion for Journalism, A Newspaper Editor Writes to his Readers
- Wah-say-lan, A Tale of the Iroquois in the American Revolution
- Wah-say-lan, Seneca Warrior

Cover caption: The author, left, and friend Jimmie Palmer rafting on the Erie Canal in Pittsford, NY.

For information, write to:
Elm Grove Press
PO Box 153
Old Mystic, CT 06372
www.elmgrovepress.org

Published 2016

ISBN: 978-1-940863-05-4

Index

In Memory of

Ann H. and James A. Smith

For Tyler and Scotty Davis

so they will know

---

and for Susan Hastings Lunt

Introduction

MEMOIRS

Oh, how memoirs have been explained, postulated, examined, right down to what is the very meaning of truth. The truth is, everyone has different memories, even of the same event. So what actually happened can be elusive. You learn this in journalism, covering an accident, for example, along with a lot of other reporters. Depending on where you stand, whom you interview, how much time you spend at the scene, your account can differ from other accounts.

Many of the people in this book have read the parts they are in and have offered helpful suggestions. In the end, I tell the story of us first Baby Boomers -- born in 1946, graduated from high school in 1964 and college in 1968, and turning 70 this year of 2016, -- the way I remember how it happened.

The writing guru William Zinsser, in his book "Inventing the Truth, The Art and Craft of Memoir," described how he and his mother had a different view of his grandmother.

"The truth is somewhere between my mother's version and mine. But (my grandmother) was like that to me — and that's the only truth a memoir writer can work with."

You will find in here a tale involving my brother Bill, my daughter Steph, our dog Jack, a big fish, and me. There is no question we caught the fish, but how we caught it after it broke the line, well, here are three fish tales: Steph remembers all three of us in the canoe, Bill remembers just him and me in the canoe; Steph remembers him "madly" reeling in his line to ensnare the broken line and bobber being pulled by the fish, Bill remembers a "Hail Mary" cast out and entangling the line that originally hooked the fish.

More than three decades later, Steph's version:

"I recall being surprised and very nervous when I was jerked into the water after the fish hooked itself. You came over (after I yelled for you), grabbed the pole, and the line snapped. I also recall standing on the old deck above the shore with you and Billy, and seeing with you guys the bobber come cruising along. Billy madly reeled in his line and hooked it, and we all got in the canoe and the carp dragged us up and down the shore until it got tired.

I don't remember much else — maybe I have a vague memory of Jack sniffing the carp. I loved being on adventures with uncles!"

Bill's version:

"OK, here is my take on the details:

- we had seen some big carp cruising so we put a set line out with a piece of baked potato as bait.
- I think you were sitting in the shade and I was milling around doing ""stuff."
- the ladies and Barbie were sunning on the deck.
- Stephie was also milling around doing "stuff," but she kept going over to the break wall where the pole was set to keep an eye on the bobber.
- I think we both heard her yelling about the same time and started towards her as she was being pulled into the water, still on her feet holding the completely bent-over rod.
- I don't recall whether it was you or me that reached her just as the line snapped, and she was NOT happy.
- I told her not to worry because "carp always return to where they were hooked" (which of course is a lie).
- we all went back to whatever it was that we were doing for half an hour or more and then you, Steph, and I started up the stairs (maybe for lunch, not sure).
- then we spotted the freakin bobber heading south along the shore about 30 feet out — we were on the first landing above the water, where someone had left a spinning rod with a spoon on it.

- I made one Hail Mary cast out beyond the bobber and reeled like mad. The spoon caught the line with the bobber attached and lodged in the bottom of the bobber.
- I rushed down the stairs with the pole in hand, playing the fish on the way and then stood knee deep in the water, trying to play it so the line wouldn't snap again.
- you went and got the canoe and paddled over and picked me up, we both took turns playing the carp while he towed us around in the canoe.
- finally, after what was probably an hour, we paddled back to shore and were able to land him.
- we were very proud of ourselves and stuck out our chests (well, you did, mine looked good already).
- when we tried to weigh the fish it immediately overloaded the 25# scale we used.
- I think I remember Jack sniffing at it, and both Kris & Sue claiming they would never swim in the lake again.
- it was one big fish, and that is the truth. (The bobber is still in my tackle box — complete lie.)"

(Readers will find my version of the big fish story in Chapter 11.)

Giving cousin Fran Zornow a ride on my first tricycle; hopping on my first bicycle.

Chapter 1

BICYCLES, SNOW SHOVELS AND LAWN MOWERS

My working life began at age 8 with a snow shovel and a lawn mower. I was saving for my first 24-inch bicycle. I wanted to ride it each day to fourth grade at Lincoln Avenue School.

It did not occur to me then that my mother, and her father before her, also went to Lincoln Avenue. What I knew is that I was leaving behind the nuns at St. Louis School, leaving behind my tiny 18-inch two-wheeler with solid rubber wheels, and heading to public school. I was going to arrive in style.

But I didn't have the $54 required for the dashing, dark red, nearly maroon bike displayed at the Western Auto Store in East Rochester, the next village over. My father had a maroon Ford, I was going to have a maroon Huffy Western Flyer. I had not quite a full year to find the money — that winter, spring and summer of 1954.

I'm talking about work for pay, not the chores you do at home. Work with a snow shovel at $2 a sidewalk could add up, eventually, to that sturdy new bicycle. Chestnut and maple trees grow tall between the sidewalks and narrow streets of the village of Pittsford in western New York State. Each house had a walk leading up to its front door. First you shovel the sidewalk along the road, then you shovel the walks up to the front doors.

You wanted the snow to be heavy for forts and tunnels and snowball wars. You wanted it to be the light, fluffy kind if you're spending your afternoons shoveling walks.

There was other work in that decade after World War II when young men were back home starting careers and families. There was helping Mom carry the glass bottles of milk from Pittsford Farms Dairy in their wire carrier up the hill and across the Erie Canal bridge. I'd warn her to "chotch out, Mom" for the oncoming cars. I was almost 3 when we first started buying the milk together. She was 24. We'd cross North Main Street at the bridge, walk down the hill, past Schoen's Alley, over the railroad tracks and up six stone steps to the dairy set back from the road with the cow barn and pastures beyond.

Families, at least families I knew, didn't have two cars back then. So, after Dad drove off to work, we walked to buy the milk. When I was a few years older, we walked upstreet in the other direction to buy the groceries, first at Hart's on the Four Corners, then at the new, big Star Market a block down State Street past Uncle Tom Dowling's Gulf station. Mom bought enough to fill two paper grocery bags. She carried one and I carried the other. Once, in Hart's, I impulsively picked a grape from one bunch as she put another bunch in our cart. I knew it was a sin to steal a grape from the grocery store but I popped it in my mouth anyway. The theft came in handy for my First Confession before my First Communion. It was the only sin I could think to confess to: grape thief.

That winter my father was pleased I'd shovel the sidewalks up to our front door and the walk to Great Aunt Una's. She lived downstairs and we lived upstairs at 25 North Main Street. It was her house. She grew up there with my grandfather as the 19th became the 20th Century. It was in 1949, the year I turned 3, when we started renting the upstairs.

It took me a few years to figure out that I could take the snow shovel around the village, knock on people's doors and offer to shovel their walks. Greg Stephany, who lived just across the canal, joined me. Sometimes we'd work together, which meant we had to share the earnings.

Other times we'd sort of divvy up the street. That meant shoveling fast because I didn't want Greg to get more houses than I did. It was my first lesson in the competitive free market.

We came up with $2 as a fair price. None of the housewives balked. My Aunt Margaret Zornow next door, my mother's oldest sister, had a long sidewalk that swung around to a side door. She paid me $3. Upstreet, behind the two blocks of stores and Town Hall and the village Post Office, was a grid of narrow side streets with modest homes on small, well-kept yards. I was stunned one day, in a storm depositing more than a half-foot of snow, when Mrs. Hoeltke handed me $5. When I got home at dark I told my mother what Mrs. Hoeltke had paid me.

"You know, Jimmy," said Mom, "you'll find that some of the most generous people are the ones with the least to give."

I shoveled my way to a little more than half the $54 I needed. I knew I had to earn it, but I found skating on the canal a lot more fun than shoveling. The state lowered the water to a depth of two feet every winter — creating a skating haven for kids in our neighborhood. If we got tired of skating, we walked to the dairy farm with our sleds. There was a perfect hill for sledding in the cow pasture. All afternoon we'd slide and slide and slide, until our legs got tired and prickly cold walking up the hill so many times.

As the snow melted and the green grass emerged that summer between third and fourth grade, I knew I needed to find a way to get that bike. It had been my job to mow Una's yard, but it was our yard too. It was merely a chore and not for pay.

Unlike carrying a snow shovel on your shoulder, I knew I couldn't push the mower around the village. But next door was the village library, where Una's sister, "Auntie," was the librarian. She told me that my cousin Timmy Dowling wouldn't be mowing the library lawn any more — he was old enough to get a real job — and asked if I would like to. She could pay me $2 each time. She was already paying me 50 cents to stack the firewood next to the fireplace in the library community room every week. Now I was into the bigger bucks, and I could use Una's heavy green reel mower with a gear that put it into forward so you wouldn't have to push it.

When I first started using that big old two-wheeled machine in our own yard, it was difficult to muscle the right wheel snugly on the grass as you mowed along the flowerbeds. Letting the wheel slip into the dirt very possibly meant damaging the tulips, daffodils, pansies, all kinds of well-cultivated flowers. But I mastered it and found that doing the library lawn was easier because there were no flowerbeds.

I also cut a deal with Aunt Margaret's husband, Uncle Ted, to mow their lawn for $3, the same I got for shoveling their sidewalks. It took a long time, counting the front yard, the side yard under the cherry trees lining the canal bank, and the backyard where we played baseball until the sun set on summer nights. It was an acre and a half. Separating our two yards was a low stone wall that ended at a white arbor, a rather ornate entrance and exit, I thought, between cousins' yards.

I was supposed to use the Zornows' mower, a rotary that you had to push, but it cut a larger swath. It was an all-afternoon job and it went fine my first time. The second time, however, I couldn't get the thing to start. I pulled and pulled and pulled on the rope but the machine just kept sputtering. I went home, dug into my stash for the bike and walked upstreet to Place's Hardware Store and bought a new spark plug. I put it in, checked the gas level and the oil level, set the choke and started pulling on the rope again.

No luck. The thing was gurgling. I probably flooded the engine. I was pulling and pulling and pulling, then sat down and just stared at it. That's when Ted came home.

"What's the matter, Jimmy?" he asked.

"I can't make it start. I've tried and tried and tried. I even bought a new spark plug," I said.

"We'll, let's see here," said my uncle. He pulled the rope and the mower whirred right into action. He smiled at me. I thanked him, hid my amazement and pushed the thing off into his lawn. Later, just before us Smiths sat down to supper, Ted was at the back stairs yelling up,

"Jimmy, Jimmy, you there?"

I went to meet him and he paid me back for buying the spark plug. As I look back, it seems I was a little older, maybe 10, when I mowed the Zornow's lawn. So maybe it was just the library mowing that brought me to my goal of $54. It's funny the specific moments, even conversation we can remember, while the flow of time can be a little fuzzier.

When the summer was almost over I told my father I had the money. "I hope that bike is still at the store" in East Rochester, I said. We drove over and there it was, shiny and sturdy and waiting for me. When the clerk rang up the bill, I didn't know about sales taxes, and I stood there frozen.

I had the $54, no more. My father paused, looked at me, looked at the clerk and dug into his pocket for the some three dollars more I needed. I thought, that's a whole afternoon of mowing, but Dad didn't ask me to pay it back.

I don't remember the ride home in that big old Ford. I just remember that I now owned the best bike in the village of Pittsford. I couldn't wait for school to start. I'd be arriving for fourth grade at Lincoln Avenue in style. It turns out that one of the first days I was speeding down the sidewalk on Washington Avenue, perpendicular to Lincoln, and happened to look down. It was a blur, but I swore I saw a four-leaf clover. I braked, walked the bike back a few steps, got down on my knees and carefully looked. My fingers parted the clover and then I saw it again. It was a four-leaf clover. I carefully picked it and put it in my pocket and pedaled off to school. How Sister Marietta, Sister Brigid and the other nuns at St. Louis would love that Irish luck charm, I thought. But I was on my way to a new school.

That beautiful maroon bike became my transportation to real and imagined destinations. Not long after I bought it, my little brother Steve won a bike in the church raffle. The pastor, Father Reddington, was so pleased with Steve's thank-you note, certainly prompted by Mom, he put it in the St. Louis Church bulletin: "Dear Father, I want to thank all of you for my bike. It is the best bike in the world. I hope our new (church) bells will make everyone as happy as my bike makes me. Stephen Smith."

A brand new 26-inch bike, bigger than mine! But I knew he didn't have the best bike in the world. Still, I was happy for him.

Together, we'd take playing cards, or sometimes baseball cards — but never a Yankees card — and attach them with clothespins so that the edges stuck into the wheel spokes, and the bikes became motorcycles as we roared off to imaginary cycle races.

On weekends, when the newly expanded Security Trust Bank parking lot was empty, just up the street, we'd pedal our bikes faster and faster into ever widening circles around the expanse of blacktop. We were then fighter pilots in our British Spitfires shooting down German Messerschmitts. And as we leaned into our circular path going round and round and we lifted our hands from the handlebars, our outstretched arms and palms became the plane's wings; and we never got shot down.

Before my new bike, there was that little 18-inch two-wheeler. The day Dad took the training wheels off when I was 4 and I pedaled all alone on the sidewalk with him trotting just behind was my first remembered feeling of victory, of conquering fear, of freedom to go. It was an absolutely new feeling, akin to climbing higher in a tree than you ever had, only better. It was as if I could take off, go places.

If I might fast-forward 25 years to when I was the father letting go of my first daughter's bicycle seat as Barbara Ann pedaled for the first time without training wheels, it whip-sawed me back to 1951. The feeling of success and adventure came flooding back. But as I stood watching my first-born steer her bicycle all alone, what trepidation I felt. There she goes, I said to myself — to where? How far? I wonder if my father felt the same.

Four-year-old Jimmy Smith in Pittsford, N.Y., proudly pedaled that little bike to kindergarten at St. Louis School and once all the way to Jefferson Road — which we considered the outskirts of the village — to visit a friend. But by fourth grade it had become embarrassingly small.

My hard-earned, $54, new maroon bicycle whisked me all the way to my grandmother's house on Eastview Terrace, definitely the edge of the village. Instead of walking up North Main to South Main past Town Hall, Dutch Earl's Barber Shop and Hicks & McCarthy's ice cream shop, left on Locust Street, right on Rand Place past Kathy Garvey's house and St. Louis School, left on Elmbrook, right on Eastview Terrace, over Jefferson Road up the hill to the last house on the left at the dead end — Nanie's house — I pedaled through those streets on two wheels and was there in minutes!

On foot it was a trek and seemed like such an adventure, but really it was less than a mile. Once there, where my cousins the Dowlings also lived, we played kick the can and softball in the street, and climbed trees, swung from vines in the woods just past the meadow and its pond filled with frogs and turtles.

I explored my village with the newfound freedom of a big new two-wheeler. I rode it to my Little League games, my mitt hanging from the handlebars. I rode it to Patty Stell's and Carol Nobles' houses hoping to get a glimpse of those two little cuties; to Mel Morgan's house across from the old pickle factory where there had been German prisoners of war. My mother worked there just out of high school during World War II. She told me once how one prisoner asked her name. He sadly replied, "Ah Anna, ya, my mudder's name vus Anna."

My biggest adventure on my bike was when Dad would put it in the trunk of his car when I'd visit my cousin Andy Conine on his farm in Avon for a weekend. We'd pedal down Routes 5 & 20 and meet his friends at an appointed place. Then, as a gang of six or eight or however many showed up, we'd ride miles and miles past corn fields and hay fields and pastures to Bullhead Pond. It had a rope swing hanging from an oak tree limb and we'd jump off the rope and swim all afternoon. Then, near suppertime, we'd ride back.

Long before those travels on country roads, before my very first bike, a tricycle, was the teeter-tot. I don't know why my mother called it that. It had four wheels and today would be called a stroller. This goes to my first memory: Mom walking me down Mitchell Road in this blue and white metal teeter-tot. It had a wooden handle above a little tray in front.

I was 2 years old. I remember crossing the one-lane bridge over the canal and coming to the railroad tracks. I remember wanting to get to the tracks; maybe I wanted to see a train. I remember the pebbles on the side of the road, and a lady coming out of a house and talking to my mother. And I'd be glad when she stopped talking, turned the teeter-tot around and we'd walk back to the little white house that she and my father rented. They rented half of it. A big boy named Jan Filer lived on the other side.

I don't remember moving about a mile to 25 North Main Street in the village when Steve was born. But I do remember walking up to Place's Hardware Store with Mom when I was 3 years old and riding back on a brand new red tricycle. All my little brothers rode it, then my daughters and even some nieces and nephews. I had to replace the wheels when my grandsons came along and also rode it. Now they are too big for it, but their little cousin Ella Smith now has the red tricycle.

I rode "the trike" for only a year because, when I was 4, my father came home with that bright 18-inch, red and white two-wheeler. So, from age 2 to age 4, I went from the four wheels of the teeter-tot to the three wheels of the tricycle and to my first two-wheeler. Then at 8 years old came my prized 24-incher that I had saved for. That bike, it turned out, was not only my major mode of transportation, it was also utilitarian, especially when it came to the paper route.

The paperboy

Chapter 2

THE PAPER ROUTE

I didn't have my own paper route, but I substituted for a neighborhood kid when he went on vacation with his family for two weeks in the summer. What I discovered, and what stays with me even now, is the absolute stillness and quiet in the early morning in the village. Sunrise is noiseless — except for the birds, so joyous in the lightening dawn.

There was the sound of my bike tires on the pavement, but there were no cars this early. Sometimes I'd catch a glimpse of the milkman, Mr. Parker, making deliveries in his truck. But he was it for other human activity. Even at the Four Corners, where there was traffic at any other time, the red, yellow and green lights changed, but I was the only one to see them.

A Rochester Democrat & Chronicle man dropped off my bundle of 54 newspapers in the pre-dawn hours. Some customers wanted their paper folded in three. Learning how to tuck the third side into the first fold, was a mystery solved. Other customers wanted their paper flat and pushed under their doormat, which meant lifting the mat and placing it carefully underneath so the paper wouldn't rip. Still others wanted the paper between their screen door and the front door. You had to get each one right. Because I did it just for two weeks, I had notes to remind myself where to put each paper for each house.

The route was upstreet, from the village center up to the high school, about a half-mile away. Almost everyone in the little houses side-by-side on Washington Avenue got the morning paper, then on to Lincoln Avenue, up the hill on Sutherland Street, where some of the homes were behind big brownstone walls, then back down to Monroe Avenue and its large houses with big front yards and long driveways.

Miss McCarthy lived on Monroe but her yard was tiny, with big evergreen bushes hiding her front porch. It was special delivering the news to her because she was my eighth-grade history teacher. I knew she thought the paper was important. And besides, she was my second cousin or something, and so I always took care to make sure her paper was delivered just in the right spot where she wanted it — folded in the hooks under her mailbox on the porch.

What I didn't like, and why I didn't have my own route, was collecting. It took up way too much time on Friday afternoons those summers in the late 1950s. You had on your belt a metal mechanical change device for nickels, dimes and quarters. It was cool pushing the levers to pump out the right change when a customer handed you dollar bills. Certainly not all of them, but a good many of those 54 housewives, once they got their change, would hand you back a dime for a tip. That was the good thing about collecting, but it was mostly a pain. Sometimes no one would be home and so you'd have to go back, even on a Saturday morning. First you'd deliver on Saturday, then go home and eat breakfast, watch some cartoons, make a decision on which ones were OK to miss — not "Mighty Mouse," that's for sure — get on your bike and knock again on the customers' doors, hoping they were home this time.

Then came the big, thick Sunday paper. Half of it was delivered Saturday night. I'd have to get up earlier Sunday morning and insert the sections from last night into the front sections that were just dropped off. But they were so big I couldn't fit them all in my bicycle baskets — two on either side of the back wheel — so I'd take half and deliver them, then ride back home, get the other half and deliver them. One Sunday when it was raining, my mother got up and drove me around the route. I felt bad for her having to do that, but she didn't seem to mind. She grew up in the village.

Mary Ann Finucane and 21, 25 and 27 North Main Street

Chapter 3

25 North Main Street

Except for the last months of World War II on Army Air Corps bases in Valdosta, Ga. and Madison, Wisc. with her bomber pilot husband, Ann Hutchinson Smith had spent her whole life in the village of Pittsford, N.Y. She was born in a squat, flat-roofed Greek revival that seems to hug the ground at 21 North Main Street. She spent her childhood two doors down at 27 North Main Street, a tall, impressive brick Victorian. She raised her sons on the second floor of the house between the other two, a wooden white Victorian at 25 North Main Street.

Revolutionary War soldiers settled the town in 1789. They built their first cabins at Big Spring, a Seneca Indian camping site. It was part of the Phelps and Gorham "purchase" of some one-third of Seneca lands. The westernmost tribe of the powerful Iroquois Confederacy, the Seneca had lived there for centuries.

Big Spring was renamed Pittsford in 1814. Three years later, New York Gov. DeWitt Clinton started digging the Erie Canal. Thirty feet wide and four feet deep, "Clinton's Folly" was finished in 1825, bringing thousands of white settlers, many of them immigrants, into former Iroquois country. More than that, the Albany-to-Buffalo canal lowered the cost of transporting goods from $100 to $8 a ton. To children in the 1950s, after it had been re-engineered and dug to a depth of 12 feet, the canal was a place to swim in and raft on during the summer and ice skate on in the winter, when the water level was lowered to two feet. In grammar school music class, we'd sing "The Erie Canal Song," written in 1905 by Thomas S. Allen:

> Low bridge, everybody down
> Low bridge for we're coming to a town
> And you'll always know your neighbor
> And you'll always know your pal
> If you've ever navigated on the Erie Canal

In my own young mind the State of New York was serving us kids with the historic canal – swimming depth in the summer, ice skating depth in the winter. In actuality, a century earlier the canal made the village of Pittsford a center of agricultural trade.

At about the same time, across the Atlantic Ocean in County Down, Northern Ireland, Samuel Hutchinson and Ann Cleland were born. They married in Ireland and had 10 children, including Samuel III, born July 22, 1856, on the family's way to America. Mary Ann Finucane was born in County Kerry, along Ireland's River Shannon, in 1859, a few years after the house at 25 North Main Street in Pittsford, N.Y., USA, was built. Sam Hutchinson III and Mary Ann Finucane met in America, married on April 4, 1883, and eventually bought the house at 25 North Main. There they raised four children: James Herbert "Herb" Hutchinson, my grandfather; Madge, Una and Sam. Sam grew up and moved to Albany. Madge married Lem Lusk and moved to a little house just over the canal bridge. Herb married my grandmother, the beautiful Leslie Grover, and moved next door into the Greek revival. Una never married and never moved. She spent her entire life at 25 North Main Street. Think of that. The same house your entire life. She was a high school history teacher in Rochester ("the city," we always called it) for nearly 50 years.

Her older brother Herb and Leslie's first child, Margaret, was born in

1907. Their sixth and last, Ann, my mother, was born in 1924 in a small bedroom on the second floor of that Greek revival. Four years later they moved two houses down to the brick Victorian at 27 North Main. There my mother grew up. Her generation grew up fast. The Japanese bombed Pearl Harbor when she was in high school. She married her high school sweetheart when he was on a two-day furlough from his Army Air Corps basic training to be a pilot. I made her a mother the year after World War II ended.

Ann Hutchinson and her husband James A. Smith would also raise four children at 25 North Main Street. Aunt Una had cut the big old home in half, creating a two-bedroom apartment upstairs. She lived downstairs. My parents moved in upstairs with my baby brother Steve and me. We Baby Boomers were the fourth generation in our family at 25 North Main Street.

The Finucanes of County Kerry spawned plenty of the growing population of Pittsford. Mary Ann's sister Katherine never married, but her sister Margaret married Morris Phillips; Anna married Isaac Hicks, Ella married John McCarthy. It goes on — my grandmother's brother, Albert Grover, married Ethel Malone, whose sister May married a Spiegel. Margaret Finucane Phillips had a granddaughter Mary who married Tom Burden. The Hutchinson, Lusk, Hicks, McCarthy, Spiegel and Burden families are all linked by blood and neighborliness over the decades in the village of Pittsford.

Chief Warrant Officer Herbert Hutchinson, the Apple Blossom Queen (Rochester Democrat & Chronicle), Flight Officer James Smith.

Chapter 4

Apple Blossom Queen

My mother, the youngest of six children, got her picture in the Rochester Democrat & Chronicle on May 22, 1942. Under a fetching photo highlighting her bright eyes and sweet smile is the headline: "Pittsford High Girl Chosen For Blossom Queen Race."

"Willowy, dark-haired Ann Hutchinson, Pittsford High School senior, yesterday was chosen 'queen' to carry hopes of the town in the Monroe County competition of the Western New York Apple Blossom Festival," the story reads. It described her: "five feet, six inches tall, she weighs 112 pounds, has gray-green eyes and dark brown hair" and reported that she'd be competing against girls from the other towns in the county, ending in a luncheon for the queens and their mothers, a procession, coronation and festival ball at the University of Rochester.

She wasn't crowned the western New York queen, but she was Pittsford's. She graduated a month later from high school and in her yearbook "Hutch" was voted "Irresistible," a "Hot Stepper," and most "Like a Date With."

All through high school she dated Jim Smith, a city kid who went to Aquinas Institute in Rochester. They met when they were 14 years old while skating on the Cobbs Hill skating rink in the city.

No matter to Paul Buholtz, who was, no doubt, one of the boys who most wanted to date Ann Hutchinson. He wrote to her in January 1944 from where he was stationed in Europe. "One nite the fellows in the hut got to discussing the pretty girls they knew back home," he wrote. "Somehow or another, I got in the discussion and I told them that I know a girl back home that would make theirs look homely. Right away they told me that I would have to prove it."

Pvt. Buholtz thought his buddies in the 11th Infantry would forget it, but "they keep pestering me all the time" and so he decided to write and ask for "a good picture of yourself. Of course you don't have to, but if you would you sure would be helping me a lot."

Then the soldier asked forgiveness "for picking on you, but as you were the first one that came to my mind, I decided I would write to you." He signed off by writing, "Please destroy this letter as soon as you finish reading it."

I'm sure she sent him a photo but, obviously, never destroyed his letter.

She had enrolled at Nazareth College for Women in Pittsford, which pleased her oldest brother Herb "Brud" Hutchinson, a graduate of Georgetown University. Though he had a pedigreed college degree, Brud joined the Army as an enlisted man. His forward unit fought all the way across North Africa, into Sicily and up into Italy. After V-E Day, May 8, 1945, they were shipped to the Pacific Theater.

He was Brud because Margaret, his 2-year-old older sister, couldn't pronounce "brother" and called him "Brudder." Brud was 15 when his youngest sister, Ann, was born. He was still Brud, though when the Army shipped him overseas he asked the family to stick with Herbert G. Hutchinson when mailing him letters.

He never once talked of the war when I knew him, and it was hard to imagine what he had seen and done on the front lines against the Germans and the Italians.

It amazed me when I first learned that this soldier, when he heard that his youngest sister was going to marry her high school sweetheart, sat down in the middle of WWII and wrote her a sensitive, sensible letter advising her to stay in college and get her degree.

He acknowledged that he did not know James A. Smith of the Army Air Corps; that he must be worthy of her, but she needs to think about her education first. I'm sure part of his thinking was that the U. S. was commissioning thousands of airmen for the invasion of Japan and who knew how many would come back? But he didn't write that.

On May 18, 1943, somewhere in North Africa, Staff Sgt. Herbert Hutchinson wrote in a fine, bold script to his 19-year-old little sister that "I trust implicitly in your judgment" but warned her, "don't over emphasize the expense (of college), money has value in — and only in — the happiness it can bring; the meaning or enjoyment of wealth is strictly proportionate to the realization of true happiness in its use. I am quite certain, and feel that you must share my certitude, that Mother could realize no greater happiness from the use of her money than to have you attain a degree.

"What is Mother's and all our happiness," he wrote, "is to have you developing and enlarging your horizons by a positive and intelligent use of your college . . . oh there's so much more to it Ann, all of which you are aware, and it seems futile on my part to write about it as, at best, I can only touch surfaces, but remember and be honest now — you are young, therefore impatient, but I give you my word, four years melt away like butter in a hot pan but those four fluid years can bring you a heritage of inestimable value for the after years.

Then he closed: "I'm certainly a long winded old cuss and you've a right to be put-out and exceedingly cross with your meddlesome brother, Brud. In my own defense let it be said that this is only my view and not to be construed as the policy of the editors. Finally, there are undoubtedly other factors which weigh heavily and will influence you in your decisions — whatever they may be I know the choice will be well made as I have nothing but complete faith in your sound judgment. Love, Brud."

At this time, in her zippered black leather notebook with her initials ACH embossed in gold on the cover, there is a page of doodles and thoughts by the college freshman:

"With the coming of spring there is always (the words here "without fail" are crossed out) a corresponding slowing down of education," Ann Hutchinson wrote in her fine script. "To the professor this is usually a deplorable fact, to the student it is unavoidable but far from deplorable.

"As a freshman, you are just on the threshold of education. You have some years ahead in which you must gather in more & more learning. Perhaps I can help you now by telling you about education, what it is, how we can get the most from it, and of what special importance it is to youth today," she wrote.

Just under that little soliloquy she signs:

Ann Cleland Hutchinson

James Alfred Smith

Mr. and Mrs. James Alfred Smith

And she underlines it three times.

Pvt. James Alfred Smith was writing letters like this in 1943:

"My dearest lover, Honey I love you and love you and love you and want you so much. Oh darling you really don't realize how much . . . I want to be with you and stay with you. Darling I want to be married and have our own house and have little Ann and Jim, more than anything in the world."

In the same letter from an air base in Miami Beach, Fla., he described seven "mental exams" that lasted from 7 a.m. to 6 p.m. "for our classification as bombardier — navigator — or pilot."

He would become a pilot. She loved and respected her brother Brud. But she was smitten. She was in love with her Army Air Corps man. My mother dropped out of college and married my father on April 15, 1944. She was 20 years old, he 19. He had a two-day pass. They had a one-night honeymoon in Canandaigua, N.Y., and then he was back learning how to be a pilot.

A month before the wedding, Brud wrote to his youngest sister: "With full confidence reposed in the both of you — I toast your happiness, say, 'God bless the both of them', and pledge you my love."

Mrs. James A. Smith eventually joined her husband, first in the South, then in Wisconsin. She wrote to her mother about the first pie she made for dessert. They were living just off the Army Air Corps' Truax Field in Madison, Wisc.

"Dearest Mom, Well I have a nice big pie sitting on the table in front of me. It really looks grand, but God knows what it will taste like. I'm very much afraid the crust is going to be tough. Just the same, I think it looks pretty nice for a first try . . . Of course, I really shouldn't be boasting because I used one of those mixes for the filling, didn't make it myself. It's lemon and I had to add egg yolks, water & salt. I think the filling & meringue (?) are okay, but I'm not so sure about the crust . . . Anyway, if you get a telegram saying your daughter and son-in-law died of acute gastric upset, you'll know what happened."

And then on a small piece of paper she writes, "Just after supper. I must write this quickly while Jim is outside. The pie was good. The crust a little tough, but not bad. And — Jim said 'Now that's a good pie! That lemon is really delicious!' I didn't let on that I didn't make the filling because he thinks it's so wonderful, so you mustn't say a word. He wouldn't believe I made it at first, & looking for proof, he wanted to see the lemon peels. I told him they were in the garbage pail. Just hope he doesn't go out & look. Love, Ann

"p.s. Don't let (her sister) Rosemary see this because she would probably tell him."

My father and his fellow B-25 pilots were flying every day, or every night. Everyone was expecting the invasion of Japan. Then Harry Truman dropped the atom bomb Aug. 6, 1945, on Hiroshima and Aug. 9 on Nagasaki. The Japanese surrendered Aug. 15. On Aug. 16 Ann Hutchinson Smith wrote to her mother:

"Well, how does it feel Mom? How does it feel to say peace instead of war? How does it feel to have people say to you, 'Don't you know there's a war off?' and to go over to Tobey's or down to Eldridges & say 'Fill 'er up!' & go down to Brown's and buy all the canned goods you want without digging around for the (ration) blue points, & to realize that you won't have to worry about the old thermostat being pushed down always — and most of all to know that Brud is only on a journey, not going to war again, and that his boat will head to America now? Well, I know just how it feels, & how you feel. It seems too wonderful to be true doesn't it, it's just unbelievable after all this time."

When America went to war, Ann Hutchinson was a 17-year-old high school girl. Now she was 21, married, relieved her husband wasn't dropping bombs over Tokyo and was yearning to get home. In one of her last letters to her mother, Oct. 24, 1945, she said there was speculation "we will all be getting out soon." She reported that my father's much-decorated brother John was being discharged, but his brother Bill "is still at Aberdeen with slim hope of getting out," and his sister Viva's husband Danny "is getting discharged, then they are going to Belgium where he is to be an attaché to the American Embassy in Brussels. Whew! What important in-laws I have!"

Jack Kinsky, my father's sister Dorothy's husband, also made it back from the war. They had a gaggle of girls including Katie, Martha, Margaret, Mary and the oldest Ellen Mayo by Dorothy's first husband. Ellen was a few years older than I was. She was a dark-haired angel on earth. Like Katie, she seemed to float with such grace through life. I puzzled over how much composure two girls could carry through teen-age hood.

My mother ended her letter by saying her husband "has decided we will name one of our sons Christopher. We're going to have 3 sons and 4 daughters."

The way it turned out was four sons, none named Christopher, no daughters, though all three younger brothers — Stephen John, William Stuart and Andrew Gregory — were supposed to be Jennifer. The Smith boys eschewed grace. We had umph.

You don't bale hay in suit coats but you can be blood brothers with cousin Andy Conine.

Chapter 5

Baling Hay

Uncle Charlie Conine had a big old wrench in his big maw of a hand. He wasn't turning a bolt with it. He was banging it, banging it hard through a torrent of words — "You son-of-a-bitch! Start, you son-of-a-bitch! Goddamn you!" But the aging, still green John Deere tractor didn't budge, didn't spring to life. We sat there on the mostly empty hay wagon transfixed at Charlie's bulging biceps, his hard chin jutting at the silent engine, the veins on his thick neck popping, his handsome 30-something face contorted in anger.

Gray, threatening clouds cluttered the blue sky. His oldest son, 10-year-old Tommy, whispered that "cut hay doesn't like rain." He swept his arm across the expanse of the hayfield studded with bales that we had begun to load on the wagon when the John Deere sputtered to an ungraceful and fitful stop.

Charlie reattached the black spark plug wires, jumped up into the tractor's seat, pushed in the clutch and turned the key. A slow "umph, umph, umph," emanated from the engine. He turned the key again. "C'mon you son-of-a-bitch!"

"Umph, umph, umph."

Tommy's brother Andy rolled his eyes. Andy and I were 9-year-old cousins and best friends. Stevie was there too, my 7-year-old brother. The Conine boys, a dairy farmer's sons, were showing the Smith boys how to load a hay wagon, and the Conines were grateful for the help.

Charlie climbed down off the tractor. He unplugged the spark plug cables. Blew into them, maybe he spat into them. He put them back on, grabbed his wrench and banged a couple of good ones on the frame — "You son-of-a-bitch!" He jumped back onto the seat, turned the key — "Umph, umph, umph, umph" — "C'mon, c'mon!" Then something turned over, then something like a big fart erupted. A plume of dark smoke exploded from the exhaust pipe sticking up in the front of the old tractor. "Grumph, Grumph" then a kind of choking sound, a gurgle gurgle, a whine. Another whine and then a low, stuttering almost purr.

"Halleluiah!" shouted Charlie. "Let's go, boys, before that rain comes!"

"He always gets it going again," Andy told me as he and I jumped off the wagon. Our job was to heft the 50-pound bales from the ground up onto the wagon as Tommy and Stevie stacked them. Charlie drove up and down the rows and rows of baled hay. As we shoved the bales onto the moving wagon, Tommy showed my little brother how to interlock them so as the tiers got higher the bales wouldn't collapse.

And as the hay got up to the third and fourth tier, it was harder and harder to shove them all the way up there. You grab them by both pieces of twine that tightly hold the bale together. Then you swing it up, now four tiers, as Tommy reached down to grab them. Six tiers were as much as the wagon could safely hold. Then Andy and I scrambled up to the top to join our two fellow farmworkers for the ride back to the barn.

As a young boy back in the mid-1950s, it was an exotic trip to get in Dad's car and ride the back roads 20 or so miles to visit our cousins the Conines. Andy and I were born two months apart the year after World War

II ended when my father came back from the Army Air Corps and Charlie came back from the Marines. Being cousins wasn't enough for Andy and me. We'd secretly and solemnly become blood brothers; never mind that we already had the same blood from our mothers, who were sisters.

Andy and I discovered a whole lot of things together. We discovered a satisfying, soaring triumph riding atop a fully loaded hay wagon. You are rewarded with a sweet scent in the heavy air that invites you to pull a slender stalk from a bale and stick it in your mouth. You suck on it, chew it. There's no other flavor like it —a kind of cross between brown sugar and falling maple leaves. You understand why cows eat it and then give out whole, rich milk.

As the tractor and wagon pulled into the barnyard and stopped at the elevator that slanted up to the hayloft door, Tommy placed a bale at a time on the machine that looked like the first uphill section of a roller coaster. Two chains with small studs sticking out of them held the bales as they were noisily cranked upward. Andy and I had scrambled up to the loft door and grabbed the bales as they came off. We stacked them interlocked, just as they were on the wagon. Then we climbed down and rode out to the field for another load. Toward suppertime my muscles ached. The field was almost empty. We were finally loading the wagon for the last time. It started to sprinkle and Charlie sped up. We had to run to keep up. He kept looking back at us and hollering "That's good, c'mon boys, c'mon!"

Just as baseball is a game of inches, farming can be successful, or not, by minutes. Does baled hay lose it nutrients or even need to be cast aside because the rain came before it could be stored in the barn? Wet hay can spontaneously combust and burn down a barn. I was unaware of the vagaries, the economic risks of making a living as a farmer, until that first day of baling hay. I understood a couple of years later when Aunt Rosemary Conine mailed an old Christmas card for my birthday with an apology that "it wasn't a good year for the crops."

But this season the hay got to the barn on time. His herd ate well and produced a lot of raw milk to sell to the dairy. A farm family shares, too. Charlie had one amazing barn cat who knew when it was milking time. She'd walk over, sit on her haunches and wait patiently as he leaned down under a cow, grabbed a "teet," as he called them, and shot a stream over to the Momma calico. She'd open her mouth and swallow it down. After a few gulps and the stream stopped, she'd lick the overflow down her neck, purring as she did it. She always seemed to have a litter of kittens. You'd see them following her around up in the hayloft.

Ah, haylofts! — places of wonderment, the scents of nourishment, the stored bales providing endless spots for hide-and-seek and instant forts in case you decided to hold off German hordes on the Western Front. We called it "WW-2." Uncle Charlie was in the Marines! My father flew B-25s in the Army Air Corps! We were proud of them! In our imaginations we were them. Here we were, kids 10 years after V-J Day, earnestly, of necessity, shooting "Krauts" and "Japs" in our bunkers in the hayloft. Or we'd head out with our toy M-1s and submachine guns, even a toy bazooka, for the woods at the very back of the Conines' 200-acre farm on Routes 5 & 20 in Upstate New York.

Guns or not, we'd run. Remember running as a kid? Running just to get to the next thing? Running just because it felt good? We'd run to a stand of young saplings maybe 20 feet high. It was great fun to keep climbing, climbing, when near the top, a tree would gently bend down and deposit you back on the ground. We'd do that over and over. I can still see Tommy, a year older and always a big kid, big muscles, big chest, hanging from a branch high above as it snapped off. He fell all the way back to the ground still holding the branch high above his head as if he were still hanging from it. When his feet hit, he stood there smiling, holding the branch. He took it in his right hand, cocked his arm and heaved it like a spear, shouting, "Hey, let's go for a swim." His sisters Kathleen and Molly were always in the thick of these jaunts into nature. We'd all holler and run for the creek, a tributary meandering through a back pasture to the Genesee River. The little creek — you could nearly jump across it — widened at a place where a huge oak tree stood. My father had painted a wooden sign in fine artistic script —The Old Swimmin' Hole — which we nailed to the tree. We spent hours jumping into that little pool, pulling bloodsuckers off our skin and jumping back in.

Andy and I were cousins, best friends and, as I said, blood brothers. One day we sat in the shade and pulled out our jackknives. You always carried your jackknife, often even to school. We each made little slits in our wrists, just enough to draw blood. Then we put our wrists together and rubbed them up and down and around, mingling our blood. When we were sure it was enough we solemnly shook hands and said we were blood brothers for evermore. When it was time for confirmation in the Catholic Church, which required using an Apostle's name, he took mine, James, and I took his, Andrew. We would grow up together.

His father was a Pittsford boy. In a story in the weekly Brighton-Pittsford Post assessing the 1941 varsity basketball team, it noted the loss of key guard Charlie "Bud" Conine to graduation. He would soon marry my mother's sister Rosemary. When my mother married my father, Charlie was his best man. The Conines weren't next door, nor even in the village, but to me back then they personified the extended family and they helped define for me what true friendship meant. I also learned for the first time, just by watching and listening to these two young couples, that you can agree to disagree. My dad served as Pittsford Democratic town chairman. Charlie was a Republican — "Whistle while you work, Stevenson's a jerk, Eisenhower's got the power, whistle while you work." Who you voted for for president never got in the way of sipping a cold one in the shade in the backyard. Laughter always rose above political debates. It was a good lesson.

Football catch with Dad, Andy and Steve wrestling in the bedroom. 25 North Main St.

Chapter 6

The Storm Windows

Apprenticeships are not always voluntary. At first I thought it was really cool helping my father bring the screens out of the barn where they had been stored all winter. We'd set them against a big tree along the driveway and spray them down with the garden hose, getting them ready to replace the storm windows.

It had been my father's job to rotate the screens and the storm windows as the seasons changed. He had been doing it ever since we moved in upstairs in 1949 when I was almost 3. Now, seven years later, he was ready to train his oldest son to take over the chore. It was nothing he announced. I just found myself at his side, his helper.

It wasn't hard changing Great Aunt Una's downstairs windows, all 18 of them. But our windows on the second floor were another matter. The screens were no big problem, but it was both a test of strength and of balance to get those heavy, wood-framed storm windows on or off. Putting them on in the fall meant first washing them and, after taking the screens off, carrying the storm windows up our old wooden extension ladder holding the window in one hand while holding the ladder with the other hand. Once you got up to the second floor you somehow had to lean over, grab the window with both hands, hold the bottom out, edge the top with its two metal hinges precisely over the metal hooks on the house and ease the storm window into place.

In the spring you'd reverse the process, lifting them off the hooks and carrying them down the ladder.

There were 14 windows upstairs — including the double-sized living room picture window — in the old white Victorian home where Una had been raised and where she still lived. Her brother Herb, my grandfather, married and moved all the way next door on North Main Street where my mother was born. Now, married to her high school sweetheart, she and Dad moved in upstairs. You looked out those windows at towering pines hugging the house, chestnut trees in the front and giant elms in the lush backyard reaching out past the old horse barn. At night soft, gold lamps lit the quiet main street of the village.

Along with paying the rent, it was my father's duty to do all the windows. I didn't know he was getting tired of the task. It didn't occur to me at age 10, when Dad first had me help, that really he was prepping me for the chore. After so many years of muscling a couple dozen windows into place twice a year, he was ready to bequeath the task to me.

He patiently showed me how to properly wash both the storm windows with a rag and Windex, and the summer screens with the spray from the hose. When he got the ladder in place at each window, he'd climb up a few rungs and have me hand him the storms.

The next spring when I was 11, he took off the storms then he'd have me climb the ladder and hand me the screens. He'd stand below as I hooked them on. That fall, I graduated to hefting a few storms up the ladder, though not the big picture window. It was easier taking the storms off than putting them on, and next spring, when I was 12 and Dad was 34, he announced that the job was now mine, that he was confident I could do it. I was really pleased he showed such trust in me.

The first challenge, which I had not anticipated, was carrying the ladder, and moving it from window to window. It was heavy and you had to be careful getting it just at the right angle near each upstairs window. I was glad he wasn't around to watch me struggle so ineptly with that monstrosity of ancient graying wood. I was also relieved that Aunt Una didn't seem to be paying any attention either.

I had no trouble at all getting her ground-floor storms off and putting up her screens. I made sure to double-check just how to swing the window up and lift it off the hooks — pretty easy with your feet on the ground. When it came time to do it at second-story height I told myself, OK, just like downstairs. But I knew it wasn't just like downstairs. So I reminded myself it was like climbing all the trees. The two big pines were right there and, heck, I climbed higher in them than the ladder could even reach. I didn't think about how I wasn't lugging a heavy window while climbing trees.

But there I was leaning out from the ladder, reaching with my right hand and pulling the bottom of the window out. Putting my left hand near the top, I hefted it up off its hooks. I didn't look down. I slowly straightened my body, switched my right hand up to the top of the window, then grabbed the ladder with my left hand and slowly descended — but not too slowly, because I didn't want to lose my grip on the window.

One by one I did it, all around the house, gaining confidence with each one as I made it down to the ground. The only one left was the living room picture window. I seriously doubted I could do it. I could always tell Dad I needed help with that one. It was twice as big, twice as heavy and I could see shattered glass all over the sidewalk below me. But he showed me how to do this. He expected me to finish the job. The only thing to do was, well, do it. I told myself that I got all the others down safely. I told myself I didn't want to disappoint my father.

I looked up at it from the ground. I climbed up, pressed my legs against the ladder, leaned out, inched the big window out, unhinged it and held onto it for what seemed a long time. I gripped it tight in my left and as fast as I could, shot my right hand up to the top. I eased my left off the window, over to the ladder and started down the rungs, gripping that picture window with my right hand as tightly as I could. Step by step, rung by rung. And then I felt the window touch the earth. I let out a sigh. I did it.

I thought ahead to the fall — it would be after my last year in Little League — I'd be carrying the storms up the ladder instead of down. It seemed to me that if I got them off, I could get them back on.

That fall, that's what I did. The job was mine.

It didn't seem at the time that my father was teaching me great lessons in self-reliance or any such thing. I'm not sure my parents discussed those matters. It wasn't "Jimmy, you learn to change these storm windows and you'll know how to stand on your own two feet." The family just sort of clicked, usually. I could be wrong; maybe Mom and Dad stayed up late talking about how to raise their sons. But nothing that I can remember was ever handed down with a message. My mother had an innate way of showing how to be and not be. All you needed to do was emulate her.

When we were younger, my father liked taking us over to the library lawn, a long swath of grass where he'd pass us a football. The former high school star would yell at us, "Go out farther, farther!" Then he'd throw that ball in a long arc into our outstretched hands.

He told me years later, after I was grown and had kids of my own, that he should have seen the goalposts when he was a standout halfback in high school.

"I just threw the ball," he said. "If I'd seen the goal, I would have been a better player."

And that was a lesson in life he never really taught because he couldn't see the goal himself. Look ahead, set a goal, achieve it   that was something he couldn't offer. So, with the storm windows when I was 12, I was certain Dad was just done with the chore and was handing it over to his oldest son. And after a couple of years I started training my younger brother Steve. Then it would be his turn. Bill, four years younger than Steve, would also get his chance at it. When Bill arrived in 1953, we'd been living in the two-bedroom flat on the second floor at 25 North Main Street for four years. Steve and I had one room, my parents the other. I overheard my mother telling my father one day, "Jim, either we buy a house or we get bunk beds."

Dad came home with bunk beds that weekend. I got the top, Steve got the bottom and the new baby moved into our room a little later. When Andy came along, it was four Smith brothers sharing that bedroom.

Andy was a breech birth. He came out backwards, as he is wont to say. His 35-year-old mother had a tough time of it. Many years later she described to us all a near-death experience where she was floating above the delivery table deciding whether to go back or not. She saw a light and people she loved in the beyond and it was enticing, but she opted to have the fourth kid March 14, 1959. Mother and son spent five days in the hospital.

Her mother, my grandmother Nanie, spent each day with us. Mom and I corresponded and she saved my handwritten letters.

"Dear Mom, I like the name you decided," began one. "Everyone is satisfied with Andrew Gregory," I assured her.

It turns out that his arrival was somewhat of a cause célèbre in junior high school. Many were cheering for, finally, a girl for the Smiths. In fact, I told her, "Everyone was disappointed in school except Bob Verbridge." Butch MacMillan was "disappointed because he wanted Jenny. Jim Tolman wanted a girl anyway."

So there I was, 12 years old and telling my mother how she disappointed everyone for giving birth to another son. I closed with, "I'll have to say good-bye because Nanie has to come and see you now. Your oldest son (of 4) Jim"

I did manage to write that "I can't wait 'till you're home so I can see you and the baby," and told her that things were under control: "I got up at 6:30 and set the table, ate, got dressed, got Dad up and went to church." I even covered for my brother: "Stevie couldn't write because he didn't have time."

In the next letter I admitted that, really, "Yesterday I would have slept the whole morning if Stevie didn't wake me up at 6:30. Today I would have slept a while too if Dominic (our yellow tiger cat) didn't come in and meow at me and told me to get up. I guess I'm just not an early bird anymore." And I signed it, "With all my love, Jim"

Perhaps these were early signs of a truthful writer. Besides, if Andy had been Jenny, well, bunk beds wouldn't cut it.

My father Jim Smith, the high school football star (Rochester Times-Union), later at work with colleague Bill Schubert (in fedora) at the East Rochester Despatch.

Chapter 7

The Youngest Son

James Alfred Smith was the youngest of eight children and by the time he was a high school football star, my mother once explained to me, his father was worn out about children. A railroad telegrapher and part-time numbers runner, he saw his youngest play in only one football game for the famed Aquinas Institute of Rochester.

My father, whose sons played soccer, was much more attentive. Yet as his family grew, his career stalled. Coming back from the Army Air Corps, he first found work on the greens and grounds at a golf club. Then he went into newspapering, first as a Linotype operator, then as an advertising artist — he had real artistic talent — and salesman — he had the gift of the gab — and later as an editor at weeklies. But these were not lucrative positions and he jumped from one small paper to another.

He took me to one of the papers when I was very young. He sat at the Linotype machine and typed my name. It was a humongous, black contraption with a long, upright arm. A bright shank of lead hung into a pot where it melted into a thick silver soup. As he typed in a cadence controlled by the machine, a hot piece of lead chugged out of the machine. Three pieces this day in upside-down-and-backwards letters that read Jim Smith, James Herbert Smith and James H. Smith.

"Don't touch them, Jimmy," he warned, "they're hot." When they cooled he took them off the Linotype and showed me. I kept them. When I became a journalist, I put them on my desk. Through 42 years of journalism I always had them on my desk. I still have them.

He and the other young men at those little newspapers managed to have some good times at work. They'd have headline-writing contests — my father's favorite winner, with the news that an elephant named Tom at the Rochester zoo attacked an employee: "Tough Tom Tusker Tramples Turd Tender." I'm not sure they actually printed it.

Dad drank too much beer and developed a weakness for poker games and horse racing. He and Tom Dowling and other young men would head for the races too many nights a week. I hated it when he'd come into the living room where Steve and I would be sitting on the floor playing and he'd say, "Jimmy, give me four numbers!" He'd be excited, his chiseled handsome face accented with a broad smile. He told me they would be his lucky numbers at the track.

"C'mon Jimmy," he'd urge, "four numbers" and I'd finally cough them out. He hardly ever won.

One night Steve and I were sleeping when I woke up to quite a racket out in the kitchen. Pans were hitting the walls and my beautiful 20-something mother was yelling. Another night Dad came home late and drunk with his brother John. Mom ordered my uncle out of the house. You could hear him say as he went down the front stairs, "Jeez, all I wanted was a ham sandwich."

Those four rooms upstairs — kitchen, living room and two bedrooms with one bath — were closing in on Mom. Too often her handsome, muscular husband sat at the kitchen table looking at the want ads in the paper, circling a few with a pencil.

One day he told me he'd been offered the job as editor of the weekly Palmyra Courier-Journal. Mom was proud of him. So was I. He took me on the 45-minute drive to Palmyra, into the downtown department store and bought me my first suit — I can't remember why, I think it had something to do with dancing school. All the kids in seventh grade were going to dancing school, and you needed a suit.

After we bought it, he showed me his office and where the papers came off the printing press. I liked that he was in charge. But a year later the job was over. He explained to Mom and me that the woman who owned it wasn't satisfied. "I increased circulation, I increased ad lineage, but it wasn't enough for her," my father said quietly, defensively, slowly shaking his head back and forth.

Unemployed again, he refused to get "relief." Unemployment compensation was for losers, he'd say, but his family was hungry. We drank milk at supper every night, but Mom started using a small orange juice glass for hers. I'd argue with her that she needed milk too, but she'd quietly say the small glass was enough. I was still earning some money mowing and shoveling. Some Friday nights Dad wouldn't be home and there was no supper, so I'd suggest to Mom that we go up to Hicks & McCarthy's. She'd let me buy sandwiches or burgers for her and my brothers. How could he do this to her? I'd ask myself.

When I was in high school I don't ever remember discussing college with my parents. I didn't even tell them when my guidance counselor my senior year said to me, "Jimmy, are you sure you want to go to college?"

That made up my mind for me. I applied to one and got in.

About this time I heard my father on the phone talking to debt collectors and later whispering to his wife that he could end up in jail, which I thought was something he shouldn't say to her. But it scared me. So I went to see Uncle Ted at his office down the street and asked him if I could borrow $800, the amount my father told the bill collector on the phone that he did not have.

Dad and Ted, an older self-made millionaire, weren't exactly buddies, even though they lived next door to each other. In fact, I remember them talking to each other only once. Anyway, Ted told me he couldn't loan me the money for my father. Then he said, "But, Jimmy, if you ever need money for college, anytime, just ask me."

I never took him up on his offer. I should have said I needed $800 for my first year. I was disappointed he wouldn't help out my father, but I was surprised and pleased he was willing to help me with college.

Finally Dad landed a job in the marketing department at Friden, Inc. in Rochester. It was his best job ever. He got letters from his boss telling him how well he was doing. "I want you to know that all your extra time and work is appreciated," his supervisor wrote, "Your concerted efforts did much to make the 18th (convention) the most successful so far — Truly it takes good men to do a better job."

He never showed me that, but my mother did.

He did tell us about meeting Elvis Presley during one of the business conventions he helped organize on a Caribbean island. "I got on an elevator and another guy was already in it. It was Elvis. I said, 'Hi, Elvis, how are you'. He smiled and said he was fine," is what my father told us.

When I was in college he took me to Friden one day just to show me around. We were going up a broad staircase from the big lobby. A janitor was sweeping the stairs. My father stopped and chatted with him. Up on the second floor, he said to me quietly, "You should always stop and pay some attention to guys on the lower rung."

That might have been when I was home from college for a weekend and, back on campus, received a letter from my mother March 9, 1965. She wrote that she wanted me to know "how sorry I am that things seemed to go wrong. The thing I look forward to most in the world is having you come home. And that goes for Dad and the boys too."

I must have told my parents about a speech course I was taking because Mom's letter was explaining why it seemed Dad had criticized a speech I gave in class. *"If he wanted to be perfectly honest, which he would with me, he would admit that he couldn't begin to write a speech as well as you. But he has to feel that he can advise you. It's completely necessary to him to feel that way. Maybe even more than in a normal situation where he would be paying for your education. It isn't necessary for him to feel that way because he needs to dominate you, or anything like that — but because he needs to be your father, and to find some reason to deserve the privilege of being your father."*

Whenever she could she'd try to explain him to me, to defend him. She wrote my junior year that Dad is proud of me. *"The tremendous pride he feels for you and all you have accomplished is something he has surely always needed. His own young years were good enough in some ways, but oh how sadly lacking in others.*

Do you know that when he took his First Communion he walked down to Blessed Sacrament all alone, and not one person in that whole big family of his went to see him? Sometimes I think that is one of the saddest things I ever heard. That's the way it was through all his years. If he has ever seemed thoughtless — it isn't that at all but simply a hangover from all those growing up years when he went his own way and nobody cared much one way or the other."

In another letter, my senior year in college, she wrote, *"Do you know your Dad is working so damned hard to get ahead? You know how much you had helped — when you never should have needed to. Believe me, he wishes to make it up to you. He works toward it. We may never make it — but you will and we are proud!"*

I don't think that was a reference to Dad "borrowing" my student loans. The first time was when I received a $500 scholarship at high school graduation. He told me he needed it. I went to the bank and withdrew the $500 in cash and gave it to him. Each semester in college I'd get National Defense Student Loans and many of them went to him. That meant I had to find more part-time jobs in college. He later did the same with my other brothers. One thing we did was pledge to never tell Mom, and I don't believe she ever knew.

It became just part of life. But it also hardened me. I don't play poker. I don't go to the races. I rarely even buy a lottery ticket. I pledged to myself I'd be successful enough to never have to do something like that. It must have bothered him, but he was a stoic man. You could never tell what was going on inside his head.

He used to show his young sons his biceps. He'd flex his right arm and say, "Look at this." We were amazed at the size of his arm muscles and we wished, hoped ours would be the same when we grew up. Mine never got as big as his.

Finally, late in life he received an inheritance from a rich aunt. He bought his wife a house — the house she had always wanted, the house they talked about having before they were married. It had apple trees in the backyard, flower gardens carefully tended by my mother, bird feeders, a small pond and a flagpole a few feet off the paved driveway. One winter night he drove home late, skidded in the snow and hit the pole, bending it to nearly a 90-degree angle about three feet from its base. His youngest son

Andy tried to bend it back up. He couldn't budge it. Dad came out, grabbed the pole just above where it was bent, and muscled it back up, straight as if it had never been hit. Andy still can hardly believe it.

After three battles with cancerous tumors, the last one got him in 2002. In his will, our father paid all his sons back many times over the value of those student loans he had "borrowed."

Starmite

Chapter 8

A New Camera

For years my mother had been taking her sons' photos with an old Kodak box camera. It was called a Brownie, which I thought was odd because it was black. She'd hold it in front of her and look down through a small viewfinder on the top of the box, get a kid in the center, then push a lever down on the side with her right thumb. It worked, and we had plenty of family photos.

But it seemed to me that she needed a more modern camera. Kodak was advertising them everywhere, in the newspapers, in Life and Look and the Saturday Evening Post, and on the Walt Disney show. Everyone was starting to use color film and I wanted Mom to have a new camera.

Just past the Four Corners upstreet, after the Pittsford Department Store, was the Central Pharmacy. It had several new Kodak cameras, displayed next to rolls of Kodachrome film. Just what she needed. I knew any "deluxe" models were out of the question. So I zeroed in on a neat little compact called a Starmite, $13 with tax, including twelve little bluish flashbulbs. I was never good at math, but I was going to figure out how to buy that camera.

My math deficiencies were becoming a concern. First Dad tried to help with my homework at the kitchen table. Then my older cousin, Dan Dowling, who everyone knew was a math whiz, was trying to show me the mysteries of algebra. It wasn't his failure to teach, it was my failure to learn or even to concentrate long enough on the puzzles of pi-r-squared.

In eighth-grade math class Mr. Gumina knew I was a lost cause. One day he walked by my desk and noticed "Pittsford" in ornate script on the cover of my notebook.

He beamed. I could see him thinking, "My God, something Jimmy Smith can do." He asked enthusiastically, "Did you write that?"

I didn't want to disappoint him, but I said quietly, "No, my dad did. He's a good artist."

The young teacher smiled slightly, put his hand on my shoulder and said, "Tell your dad, nice job."

My cousin Frances Zornow, next door, began sacrificing one evening a week to save me from failing math. We were told that we were going to a tutor. I knew Fran didn't need a math tutor, but I went and still couldn't learn algebra and I always thought Fran was real gracious to go along with the ploy. I was pretty sure her mother, my mother's oldest sister Margaret, paid for the tutor.

Margaret would be the key, ultimately, to my buying the camera. It was late fall and mowing lawns was slowing down. Christmas was coming, but who knew when it would snow for shoveling walks. So I came up with a plan — my lunch money. My parents gave me 35 cents each day for hot school lunch, with a dime for an ice cream sandwich for dessert. I decided to live on the ice cream sandwiches, allowing me to save 25 cents a day toward the Starmite. That meant I saved $1.25 each week. I figured that in eight weeks I'd have $10. I was more than ready for supper those weeks in eighth grade.

It was almost November and neither the library lawn nor Aunt Margaret's yard next door needed mowing. Snow came the second week in December, but I was on the eighth-grade basketball team and practicing every day so there was no time for shoveling walks. I started to worry that someone would buy the camera before I did. What did I know about more than one in stock? I knew Mr. Way at the pharmacy. Just before Christmas I went in to try to strike a deal with him. I asked if I gave him the $10 I'd saved and the rest by the end of the year, could I take the camera now? I told him it was my gift for my parents. We went over the price and he told me I would owe him three more dollars by Dec. 31. I asked if it came with a roll of film.

The white-haired gentleman had a kindly face. He smiled and said that it does come with one roll of color film. And he agreed to the deal. I gave him ten dollars. He put the camera in its yellow and black Kodak box and with the roll of film put it in a Central Pharmacy brown bag. I carried it home and hustled right into the bedroom, got some Christmas paper, wrapped it right then and hid it in the closet. I'd put it under the tree Christmas Eve.

Even though Dad hardly ever took pictures, I made the card out to both him and Mom. It sure made a great gift Christmas morning.

"Why, Jimmy, how on earth did you do this?" asked Mom. I just smiled and shrugged. Later, when we all had opened our presents, she carefully read the instructions and loaded the film into her new camera. She got some really good Christmas photos.

In my calculations, I had forgotten about vacation, which meant I wasn't saving my lunch money. We always wanted a white Christmas, but this year I really needed snow to shovel. And it turned out to be a white Christmas. On a day off from basketball, I shoveled Aunt Margaret's walks and she paid me the usual $3.

So before Dec. 31 I walked up to the pharmacy and handed Mr. Way what I owed him. He thanked me and said he heard my mother was pretty surprised by the gift. And, no, he didn't let on about our payment schedule.

See, what you do is pack this into a ball and throw it at moving objects.

Chapter 9

Throwing Snowballs at Cars

At Christmastime 2012 we were in Pittsford and I was riding in the car with my daughter Barbara Ann's family. I launched into some tale of my childhood. When I was done, my 9-year-old grandson, Scotty, said, "Bip, you have so many stories. They can't all be true. Especially that one about throwing snowballs at cars and then running to hide under a bush."

"Want me to show you the bush, Scotty?" I said.

I like my grandson's skepticism and I wondered whether the big forsythia bush was still in Steele's backyard. We didn't go look, but I assured the boy that all my childhood stories are true. I suppose if someone else was remembering out loud, it might be different because everyone has different memories and different perspectives on the same events. Greg Stephany might tell this differently.

There was this huge forsythia bush covered with snow, probably in the winter of 1957 when he and I were 11 going on 12. The thin and flexible branches bent easily under the snow and the bush resembled an igloo. It was seemingly impenetrable.

We were bored. It was past dusk. The streetlights had blinked on. Big snowflakes were lazily falling as we walked along the sidewalk on Monroe Avenue a block from my house. Earlier that day we had cut through backyards and passed the igloo-like forsythia bush.

We made some snowballs and were waiting for the right car to come along. A proper attack required that you hold a few on your left arm against your chest and grab and throw them in quick succession. This evening we chose the wrong target. As the car went by, it took several direct hits and then came screeching to a stop.

Four big guys jumped out, yelling. I heard, "You little bastards!"

We ran, ducked behind a line of bushes at the front of Steele's yard. We had a good jump on them and they didn't see us get through the bushes. The big snow-covered forsythia bush was up ahead. Beyond that was my own backyard, but I wasn't sure we could make it that far.

"C'mon," I whispered, "go for it," and pointed to what I hoped would be a perfect hiding place. Greg nodded and quickened his pace, taking the lead. It was darker in the yard without streetlights but those guys soon were back on our trail.

"You little shits are dead!" I heard and dove right behind my friend in under that big bush.

We could hear their stomping footsteps getting closer. They ran by and then the worst thing happened. Greg started laughing.

"Shh, shut up!" I whispered.

But I guess he couldn't help himself. I jumped on him and stuck my gloved hand over his mouth, but his body was shaking with laughter.

I could hear them coming back and they were real mad, first about their car getting hit, second, I presumed, for losing track of their prey.

We could hear them circling around the bush and I was sure they'd see our tracks right up to it. One of them, in fact, said, "They're in there! I know it."

They started rattling the bent-over branches and clumps of snow began to fall on us. I was still holding Greg against the ground with my glove across his mouth.

"We're going to kill you, you little shits!" they kept shouting and threatening.

But I guess big kids old enough to drive cars didn't want to be bothered with plunging in under a snow-covered bush.

Finally one said, "To hell with it. C'mon. We'll be late."

"We can't let these little brats get away with this!"

"C'mon, the car's parked on the side of the road."

Finally, we heard them trudge off. But I whispered to Greg, "Shh, they might come back. And don't laugh!"

"I couldn't help it," whispered Greg.

"Shh."

We waited a good while and then crawled out. We walked through the backyard to my house and then Greg went over the canal bridge to his. After that we made sure never to throw snowballs at cars with teenagers in them. Throwing snowballs at cars was as natural back then as sledding down a hill. When snow fell, it was second nature to make snowballs. Then you looked for moving targets.

Tim Dowling mowing the library lawn. Building blocks with Steve and Bill. Cowboys with Greg Stephany.

Chapter 10

Backyards

The property lines blurred for us kids playing in the library lawn, our house, and the Zornows': 21-25-27 North Main Street in the village of Pittsford. The space was transcendent. We could be Tarzan of the Apes in the cherry trees. The rope swing on the big walnut tree could fly us to the moon; no one had been there yet. The thickets of lilac and forsythia bushes could be hedges to "army crawl" along while carrying our M-1s, sneaking up on Germans. We built not one, but two tree houses. The blacktop driveway and basketball hoop on the Zornows' garage hosted endless one-on-one or two-on-two games. We turned the second floor of Una's barn into a basketball court where we could play inside all winter. Home plate became the spot of dirt worn in the lawn first at the library, until Tommy Conine lined a drive through Mr. Wadhams' garage window. So a new spot of dirt developed in the Zornows' backyard where we'd lose hardballs at dusk because they weren't white enough to see in the bushes. Jimmie Palmer always hit them way into the bushes.

To say those backyards were an enchanted land for young kids is like saying the Elysian Fields really exist — right behind our homes. Our combined yards were not quite three acres, but they offered endless adventures. Just past the row of cherry trees were the steep banks of the Erie Canal, called the Barge Canal in the 1950s. I didn't think of the banks as a boundary, but as an invitation. In the summer we swam, fished and rafted on the canal. In the winter we skated, played ice hockey and speared ugly giant salamanders called mudpuppies.

Just running out onto the Main Street bridge when a tugboat came along pulling or pushing a barge became a time-warping experience. If you looked directly down at the barge as it passed below, what happened was incredible — it wasn't moving, the bridge was, and you could imagine places you were traveling to. If there wasn't a barge in sight and we had our bathing suits on, we'd jump off the bridge into the cool, but oh so muddy water.

It was the carp that my little brother Steve and I were mostly interested in as far as wildlife in the canal went. They grew to a huge size, especially just down Schoen's Alley to Uncle Ted's grain mill. His son, our older cousin Teddy, showed us how to make "dough balls" out of Karo syrup and flour. You'd put the rounded concoction around the hook and it wouldn't dissolve in the water. It was great carp bait. We'd catch several eight- to 10-pound carp on just about any lazy afternoon.

One day when Steve was only about 4 years old and I was 7, we went down the bank to a little dock on the canal. Even at that age Steve was devoted to fishing. Sitting on the dock sometimes you could see the carp rise, and that day we saw a few big ones. We were both sitting there holding our poles when Steve hooked a lunker. The drag on his reel was tight and he was little. Before I knew it, he went flying off the dock and into the canal. But he wouldn't let go of his pole and the fish was pulling him out.

I jumped in, grabbed him around the waist and pulled him back to the edge of the water. He was still struggling with his pole bent to the max. Then the line broke, everything went calm and we sat there, soaked and laughing. When we got home, Mom wasn't pleased.

Yet she was ever so patient with our exploits. Steve would sometimes want to show her his catch — we'd never eat a fish out of the canal, especially a carp, but he wanted to show her. He'd struggle up the stairs at 25 North Main Street to our apartment proudly displaying his catch. Sometimes she'd let him keep it in the bathtub, which got interesting when Dad came home.

"Hey, get this carp out of here!" he'd holler. Steve would get a stringer, put it through the fish's gill, lug it back to the canal and let it go.

Out past the village stood the canal stopgates. Kids loved to jump off the top, higher than the Main Street bridge. Daredevils. Not me, though. I suppose some of those kids thought I was chicken, but I would jump only from halfway up the metal ladder of that big black monstrosity that I vaguely understood could be lowered for flood control. The thing was out of proportion to its bucolic setting among fields, woods and the man-made waterway it hovered above like some archaic monolith deposited there by an alien race.

One day, probably the summer between eighth and ninth grade, a bunch of us were at various levels of this humongous contraption — Ray Wallman, Mel Morgan, Fred Dehmler, Paul Selke, Tom Cook, Dave Nash, if memory serves. Suddenly one of them yells, "Hey, look at that snake!"

There slithering through the water was a huge black snake, at least eight feet long. Someone yells, "C'mon, let's get it!" Everyone jumped in. Everyone but me. I wasn't much for chasing snakes. It was quite a sight — a half-dozen boys swimming as fast as they could in pursuit of their prey. The snake didn't break its leisurely pace. It just disappeared. I had a vision of it emerging from the dark water and squeezing a boy down into the depths. But nothing happened. There was some chatter like, "Hey, where'd it go?" The kids treaded water for a while and then swam back. That ended the swimming that day. It was also the last time I ever went to the stopgates.

We were always outside except during Saturday morning cartoons on television, "Mighty Mouse" being my favorite. Just before lunchtime came "Sky King" (not a cartoon, but he had a niece, Penny — the first time I ever took notice of tight jeans on a girl). TV was new and all in black and white. One day when my father took us to the downtown Rochester Sears & Roebuck store, up the escalators to the toy department, there on the shelf was Howdy Doody with red hair, red bandana and a blue-and-white-checkered shirt. Who knew?

Rainy days could keep us inside in those Howdy Doody years of young childhood. But it wasn't all television. As Steve and I grew bigger and rougher we wrestled so much in the living room that Una took to rapping a broom handle against her ceiling, the signal to Mom that it was time for the boys to calm down. But that was a hard thing for growing boys to do.

Mom could get exasperated. Every once in awhile, she'd grab her dish towel and holler, "You little divils!"

That would be our signal to run down the hall into our bedroom, jump on the top bunk and squeeze back against the wall as Mom came rushing in swinging her dish towel.

"You little divils!" she'd repeat. But she couldn't reach us and we'd all end up laughing.

Then one day Dad came home with two pairs of boxing gloves, Jack Dempsey models. He hauled us up the attic stairs and told us to start moving stuff to the sides. He took a rope and made a square ring. He put the boxing gloves on our hands, put us in the ring and said start boxing. He showed us roundhouse-punches and how to protect your face with one glove while jabbing with the other.

Then he said that he better never hear again about any rough-housing in the living room — the room that had been Mary Ann Finucane's and Sam Hutchinson's, my great-grandparents', bedroom. That attic could get hot in the summer, but Steve and I became pretty good boxers. It didn't occur to me that Dad was solving a problem and at the same time teaching us a new sport. Some fathers back then would have just walloped sons rough-necking in the living room. We got new boxing gloves out of the deal, plus learned how to use them.

There were more-placid endeavors indoors. Crayons, watercolor paints and white paper could keep us busy for hours. There were blocks for building castles. Lincoln Logs (though not so much Tinker Toys) were the perfect complement to Alamo and Fort Apache sets complete with Rin-Tin-Tin dog figurines. And army men; literally armies of little rubber/plastic men in green or brown WWII uniforms stood, crouched or lay down firing their weapons. We had them deployed all over the living room floor. We made our own sound effects. They were our own violent video games, and nobody then did any studies on how army sets could make boys violent.

But Ann H. Smith, who had prayed for a brother fighting in Europe, and who had prayed her new husband would not pilot a bomber over Japan, took out a pen and paper and wrote this as a young mother, after Bill came along:

With summer almost at an end,
On a rainy, miserable day;
I've the dubious pleasure
Of being 'cooped up',
With three little boys at play!

Have you 'ere heard the sounds of battle —
A wild and furious foray,
As imagined and interpreted
By three little boys at play?

No jet could take off with such a blast,
No fighter dive with more whine,
No "ack ack" gun could ever compete
With those three little boys of mine.

And the bombs fall with more
Of a deafening roar
On my living room floor
Than ever before —
In any real war —

Dear God! Hold protecting hands above
Those three little heads I so dearly love!
Let them never work harder, at the business of war,
Than they are there now,
On the living room floor,
On this rainy day — at summer's end,
Three little boys
So soon to be men.

When my father got home from work and he had to step carefully in his own living room, he'd simply proclaim, "Boys, pick this stuff up." That was the worst, putting them all away in their cardboard boxes and stuffing them in the closet until the next rainy day.

Maybe it was the way you linked Lincoln Logs together that engaged our attention — avoiding the directions and building however you wanted to. Or maybe it was the imagination while building them — my mind would wander out onto the prairie or the forest where I'd be building real log cabins and real fences. I never knew my grandfathers, but now, decades later, I get out Lincoln Logs with my two grandsons if it's a rainy day. Tyler, three years older than Scotty, eventually grew out of playing with them. One day Scotty and I were playing with them and he matter-of-factly asked, "Hey Bip, when I'm not here do you play with Lincoln Logs?"

"Of Course I do, Scotty."

"Bip, you're nuthin' but a big kid!" he proclaimed.

Damn, it's fun building Lincoln Logs with your grandson.

Back in the 1950s, even "The Mickey Mouse Club" was in black and white at first, and all those early westerns: "The Lone Ranger," "Hopalong Cassidy," "Wild Bill Hickock," "The Cisco Kid," "The Roy Rogers and Dale Evans Show," "The Tales of Wells Fargo," "Death Valley Days," "Davy Crockett." They all held our interest, but mostly we found our own fun outdoors, being Davy Crockett in our ubiquitous coonskin caps, or "riding" Roy's golden palomino Trigger, or yelling "HiYo Silver! Away!" and galloping off on the Lone Ranger's white steed.

Maybe "Davy Crockett and the River Pirates" inspired my friend Jimmie Palmer and me to build our canal raft. My father agreed to drive us out to Pat Plane's farm where we picked up four 8-foot fence posts each about a half-foot thick. We bought some boards at the lumberyard on Schoen's Alley. Dad actually paid for all this. We dumped it all in the driveway and he showed us how to space the posts and then nail the boards on top. We were good to go.

We fashioned a couple of oars from scrap wood, carried our new raft across the yards and down the bank. We took off our T-shirts and sneakers, rolled up our pants and pushed off for our maiden voyage. Jimmie got on one side, I got on the other and my mother took our picture as we paddled down the Barge Canal. It was something new to do and we spent a good amount of time on that raft.

One day it was missing and we knew right away that some older kids had stolen it. Jimmie and I set out in search. Maybe it was instinct, but we walked east heading out of the village. At the State Street bridge we climbed down the bank and found our raft under leaves and branches. Our paddles were there too. We pushed it into the water, but hugged the bank as a barge went by. The men in the tugboat waved and we waved back.

We were ready to do battle if the thieves showed up. Jimmie was tough, scrappy, and I knew we'd give them a good fight. We paddled to the Zornows' dock without seeing any raft thieves. We felt victorious and hauled our raft partway up the bank and chained and locked it to a tree. It was never stolen again.

In the winter the state dropped the water level down to a depth of only two feet. We shoveled off the nearly ever-present snow to make a hockey rink. We also could set out on an adventure and skate the two miles west to the "wide waters" just past the Clover Street locks, an expanse that opened to what seemed like an endless tundra for racing, ice tag, or just letting your mind wander to wintery parts unknown. My next-door cousin Frances Zornow and I would skate out there together. The sense of timelessness was palpable. A world of just kids, letting our ice skates speed us through fresh icy air under expansive bright blue skies.

Back at North Main Street, our hockey rink attracted a competitive coterie of kids from other neighborhoods. We'd make goal "nets" out of U-shaped piles of snow. Butch MacMillan and Mike Spiegel from upstreet, Bobby Heffer and the Connors brothers from downstreet would arrive and we'd do battle, sometimes bloody-lipped battle, until darkness came and it was time to get home for supper.

No matter the season, growing up on North Main Street meant spending a lot of time on that canal. And when you climbed up the bank, there were the cherry trees.

Fran Zornow, Greg Stephany, Steve and I would spend hours in those trees when the cherries ripened. They were delicious. Some of the trees produced fruit that was a mix of deep yellow and pink, which were a tad more tart than sweet. Succulent deep red cherries grew on the other trees.

One day in the summer between sixth and seventh grade I was sitting on our back porch with great Aunt Una and her sister, Auntie. In my mind, they were old ladies, very nice old ladies. It never really occurred to me, then, that these two sisters grew up at 25 North Main Street and now they were watching us grow up there too.

The kids all called her Auntie, the adults called her Madge, short for Margaret. She married Lem Lusk and moved to the little white house on the other side of the canal bridge. Just after the turn of the 20th Century, Lem was a husky, athletic young man who rode the first motorcycle in Pittsford. He was the town constable. He also was a horse aficionado. Nearly half a century later he was still running a horse on a sulky track on the Pittsford-Palmyra Road where the Post Office now sits. He kept the dark brown gelding in the barn in back of his house. His grandson, Bill Bruce, and I would watch him work with a hammer, anvil and bellows, pulling horseshoes out of a bed of hot coals and shaping them to perfectly fit the horse's feet. It amazed me to watch him nail them onto the horse's hooves.

As an old man he was bent over, but you could still tell he was once a bruiser. He'd walk slowly over the canal bridge up the sidewalk to our house and he'd ask in his gravelly voice, "Hey, boys have you seen your Auntie?"

More often than not, she'd be on the back porch with her sister or they'd be sitting in white wicker chairs in the backyard drinking iced tea sprinkled with mint leaves picked from the garden. One day they asked me if the cherries were ripe and I told them they were.

"Instead of eating them in the trees, Jimmy, take this basket and bring it back full, OK?" Una said.

I never argued with Una and went off to pick cherries. It was really hard not to eat them as I picked, but pretty soon I had a basket full, climbed down and walked back to where she was reading the newspaper on her back porch.

"We're going to make a pie," she said, and told me I needed to pit every cherry. That meant pinching each one, making sure the pit went in a bucket and the cherry into a bowl. Both Una and Auntie supervised. Then we walked into Una's kitchen and I watched them mix flour, water, pure white Crisco from a blue can, some salt and roll a fine crust into a pie tin.

We added some sugar and a little syrup to the cherries and stirred them gently in the bowl, then ladled them over the crust in the pie tin, laid another swatch of crust on top and into the oven it went.

We ate it outside that very afternoon. Homemade cherry pie, a lesson and a real treat.

The following spring in seventh grade, for some reason there was a pie-baking contest — the boys baked, the girls judged. My grandmother, Nanie, was supervising me in the kitchen at 25 North Main. She wouldn't do the work but she was a reassuring adviser as I made the crust. It was too late for fresh cherries, so we bought a can at the supermarket.

After watching Una and Auntie make a pie, and with Nanie there, I figured I had a pretty good chance. I can't remember who won — probably heartthrob Butch MacMillan. But I came in second, which I thought was pretty good. I heard that Roberta Crump had something to do with that. Butch and I would compete at many more things than pie baking, but the next year we joined forces politically.

In eighth grade he asked me to run for office with him. He was a candidate for president, I'd be running for secretary-treasurer and Freddie Gramlich, who was just back from Africa where his father was in the diplomatic service, was our vice presidential candidate. We were required to campaign and make signs. We played off our initials — "MacMillan — Gramlich — Smith — Makes Good Sense." My father created a poster with the "Makes Good Sense" coming down off the first letters of our names.

I can't remember whom we were running against, but we won. I'm sure it was on Butch's good looks and popularity, and Freddie's return from faraway places. There we were, running the Pittsford Junior High School student government.

Herb Hutchinson and daughter Ann circa 1930 Bill, Jim, Steph, Smith 1980 and canoe-towing carp.

Chapter 11

Canandaigua Lake

Some 25 miles south of Pittsford is Canandaigua Lake, the legendary birthplace of the Seneca Indians, part of the once-powerful Iroquois Nation. Canandaigua translates into "the chosen spot," where the Seneca had lived for centuries.

It is one of the Finger Lakes in central and western New York — long, narrow, deep bodies of water carved out 10,000 years ago by the retreating glaciers.

In the Revolutionary War the Seneca were British allies. With the American victory the Iroquois were forced to give up their homelands. In 1788 the Seneca sold about 1.2 million acres from roughly Seneca Lake to the Genesee River, to Oliver Phelps and Nathaniel Gorham for $10,000, though they received only about $5,000. Profits were to be made.

Among the oncoming white settlers were Simon and Israel Stone, who founded Pittsford in 1789 with their purchase of 13,000 acres for about $5,000.

Nearly a century later, during the nation's centennial in 1876 (and the year Custer lost to the Sioux at the Little Big Horn), some men formed a partnership and built a cabin on the eastern shore of Canandaigua Lake. Upstate New York winters are cold and the lake occasionally freezes solid, as it did in 1876. It's family folklore that the partners brought the lumber in horse-drawn sleds across the lake and that Morris Phillips, who married my great-grandmother Mary Ann Finucane's sister Margaret, helped build Fisher's Cabin. My grandparents Herb Hutchinson and Leslie Grover honeymooned there in August 1906.

Growing up in the 1920s and '30s my mother spent her summers at Fisher's Cabin. Herb and Leslie's youngest daughter regaled her own boys with stories of the lake:

"I'd be out in the rowboat with my dad when one of those big thunder and lightning storms would rise over the hills on the western shore. You could see the storm heading across the lake and I'd yell at my father, 'Hurry, daddy, hurry!' But he'd just slowly row his boat. When the bow finally touched the beach, I'd jump out and scurry up the path to the cottage, but he'd slowly pull the boat up on the beach, then casually walk up the path. He'd sit in his rocking chair on the porch, ask for his pipe and rock as the wind and rain and lightning and thunder passed overhead," my mother delighted in telling us.

The porch is a marvel in itself. Logs hold up a roof, smaller logs form a railing around it. The back wall of the porch is taken up with intricate carvings of initials and dates. Inside on the south wall is a big stone fireplace and just beyond is a set of stairs leading up to bedrooms on the second floor. All the walls are the original lumber. Downstairs is a large kitchen, opening to the main room with a large dining table and the fireplace at the far end. An ornate lamp has always hung in the center of the room, with moths at night flitting around the soft glow from the round white glass with purple and pink flowers painted on it.

The cottage has a distinct, soothing aroma like oak leaves on a forest floor, and in fact it is surrounded by an oak and hemlock forest. The lake never left my mother's soul. How wonderful it must have been to spend her childhood summers there.

Her oldest sister Margaret and husband Ted Zornow bought the cottage in 1941. Nearly a decade later, Mom would take us to visit, creating some of my earliest memories — the lapping of waves on the shale beach, finding and collecting fossils at the edge of the water. My 4-year-old brother Steve got so excited once that he left the car carrying his fishing pole, ran down the path, across the porch, down the path to the beach, onto the dock and right off the end of it. Cousin Betsy dove in and brought him up. He was still clutching his pole.

We'd swim and fish on the lake and hike in the 15 acres of woods they owned and listen to Margaret and Nanie tell tales of when the Seneca Indians lived right there. The beaches are made of round flat pieces of gray shale that you could skip across the surface of the lake with a flick of your wrist. We'd have contests on who could get the most skips out of a piece of shale. On the Fourth of July, Teddy lit off fireworks.

We never got to spend a whole month or more on the lake, like our mother, but sometimes we were invited to spend the night with the Zornows. Fran and I were the same age and spent hours together. Her older sister Betsy was always willing to take us water skiing with their big Lyman inboard, and Teddy loved taking Steve fishing out in a rowboat. They became lifelong fishing buddies. Part of it was emulating our grandfather who was a legendary fisherman. Most of his 25 grandchildren never knew him. He died in 1942 before most of us were born. But James Herbert "Herb" Hutchinson was the family icon. I am James Herbert and my younger cousin is James Herbert Hutchinson, my uncle Jack and Aunt Jean's son. Like Teddy and Steve, Bill and Andy Smith, James Herbert Hutchinson still fishes the lake. He goes down deep trolling for lunker lake trout, and though zebra mussels have now decimated the fish population, James still reels in those big trout.

As kids, when it was time to leave Fishers cabin, every once in a while my father would stop for dinner at Burke's Restaurant on Main Street in Canandaigua where my oldest cousin Margaret Mary Zornow worked as a waitress during her college years. One night my father must have been flush. He ordered my first lobster tail dinner. I thought I was in food heaven.

Those visits to the lake were likes gems, islands of pure summertime bliss. But it was clear the cottage was the Zornows' and we were visitors. Years later, after I moved to Connecticut, I asked my mother if we could come back and spend a week at Fisher's. Well, it turned out we could pitch our tent on the property. For a few nights, my young wife and I, our baby daughter Barbara Ann, my mother and my youngest brother Andy, who was 12, and our little brown and white mutt Yogi vacationed there in a tent. My mother would never complain, but it must have pained her that the cottage she grew up in was empty, a few steps away.

Later, it passed on to Teddy and his wife Marcia, and they occasionally have hosted family picnics where a lot of us gather and reminisce.

I've always gone home to Pittsford and environs every summer. My first decade in Connecticut, after the tenting vacation, I'd rent cottages on Canandaigua Lake, where I taught my own daughters how to swim and fish. Steph in particular would want to fish and fish and when we hit a school of perch, she would get so excited, pulling one in after another. She loved to clean them, inspect their stomachs to see what they had eaten, but she never enjoyed eating fresh grilled perch, trout or bass.

Zenta Blumenau did. The first cottage we rented was owned by Zenta and her husband Leonid, Latvian immigrants who owned two small cottages side by side on East Lake Road. They would sometimes stay in the smaller place while we were there and each evening we'd sit in lawn chairs and watch the sun set over the green hills on the western shore. A golden path of sunlight crossed the surface of the lake.

Almost each day Zenta went out in her rowboat and caught sunfish, blue gills, rock bass, and made a delicious fish stew. Steve and I would hop in our boat with its 12-horse outboard and head a couple miles north to the waters off Fisher's Cabin. We'd inevitably come back with a stringer of big small-mouth bass.

Zenta would demand: "Vhere you get dose fish! Vhere, Vhere you get dem!"

We always gave her a couple and she was mightily pleased.

My parents, my brothers and their girlfriends, a few of my old friends would visit. My cousin Andy Conine would join us every summer. He and I and our mutual friend Fred Harrington would smoke pot, wait for the stars to come out and sit at the end of the dock serenading the waves. Both Andy and Fred played guitar and had great singing voices. I'd sort of wail along. Those were such bonding moments for three young men.

Renting nice places was fine, but as we got older Steve and I began to look for our own "chosen spot." He and Mom got into his motorboat and started cruising parts of the lake. About halfway down on the east side there are cliffs called the high banks. Hundreds of cottages lined both sides of Canandaigua Lake, but there was virtually no building on the high banks in the late 1970s.

Steve called me one fall day and said, "Mom and I found the spot." It was a wooded acre and a half at the top of the cliff and 244 feet of lake frontage about a mile south of Fisher's Cabin. We had our spot — thanks to Humphrey Bogart. His parents had a place on Seneca Point, across the lake. One day when he was 14, he may have been on the deck of a steamboat, and saw a small boy thrashing in the water. Bogart dove in and brought 3-year-old Arthur Hamlin to safety, probably saving his life. Hamlin grew up to be president of Canandaigua National Bank, and he owned the 1.5 acres on the high banks that Steve found for sale. We bought it from him in 1978 for $5,000, each of us paying $2,500.

Bill and Andy were too young and too poor to pitch in, but they helped Steve and me build a small cottage near the top of the cliff overlooking the lake. Originally we climbed up and down on ropes and homemade ladders set in a gully. Next door to the north there was a one-room cottage on the beach that we eventually bought, giving us a total of four and a half acres and some 430 feet of beach. Later we were able to get a professionally built set of stairs from the beach to a solid, set-into-the-gully landing halfway up the cliff. Smith brothers-built stairs ascend the rest of the way under towering hemlocks. All told, 138 stairs from bottom to the top.

Mom and Dad would visit most of the days we vacationed there. They would sit on the porch in the peace and quiet of our woods with a grand view out over the lake. Dad would lift his beer and proclaim, "I wonder what the poor people are doing today?" For Mom the serenity was a balm; she was on her lake again, on land owned by her sons.

The tastiest fish in the lake are rainbow and brown trout, though my father favored perch. The biggest fish are carp, bottom feeders that look like torpedoes when they glide by just past the end of the dock in about eight to 10 feet of water. We would sometimes put a piece of potato on a hook and throw it out, dangling near the bottom off a bobber, leaving the pole on the beach.

And now, the final and definitive version of the tale of catching the big carp — that is, my version:

One day I was reading on the shore when I heard "Help! Help!" I looked over and saw my 10-year-old daughter Steph holding the bent-over pole and being pulled into the water. My brother Bill and I ran over. He grabbed the pole and started pulling in, then snap, the line broke.

"Holy cow, that is one big fish!" he proclaimed. He and I went up the first set of stairs to a landing and were just chatting when he said, "Look! It's coming back! See the bobber on the water?" and he pointed out a little to the north.

Sure enough, there was the bobber floating on the surface and moving toward us at a steady clip. Bill ran and grabbed his fishing pole, waited for the right angle and then cast out at the bobber. He had great accuracy that moment. His line entangled with the bobber and the original line, still hooked in the carp's mouth. The fight was on again.

The canoe was right there. I pushed it into the water, Steph hopped in, Bill got in the front seat and I started paddling. His line was taut and the fish led the way. I couldn't turn the canoe and so we just let that carp pull us around the lake. Bill held it steady. We didn't want the line to break again. We went for quite a ride when finally he could feel the fish tiring. I was able to slowly turn back toward our shore. It was more than 20 minutes when the bow hit the beach. Bill jumped out, Steph too. Our golden retriever, Jack, ambled over to see what all the commotion was. Bill steadily reeled in the line and finally we saw the fish. It was huge. He got it up to the edge of the water, where I grabbed it under its gill but could hardly lift the monster.

We tried to weigh it, but the scale instantly dropped to its maximum 25 pounds. After Bill got the hook out of its mouth, I pulled the carp up with both hands and we got a picture of the prize. None of us would think of eating carp, so, with Jack sniffing it, I put it back down in the water, held it there for a moment, then we watched it glide away back into the depths. That's one fish story that has been told and retold in our extended family.

I moved to Connecticut in 1971 and one benefit was letters from Mom. One arrived with a photo of the lake. She suggested that I peek at it "when you feel blue" and remember that, "unlike so many things in our lives, this treasure is always there. Even as I write, even as you read, it is there. For as long as we can possibly be, it will be there. And in every way we know it — we can see it, smell it, feel it, hear it — so it is ours! Love, Mom"

There have been times when we were all there — our parents, the four brothers, their wives and children; we'd be upwards of 30 Smiths at our own piece of heaven on earth. You really can't put a value on an extended family meeting at the same place every summer, especially when you know five generations have been there. Six, actually: My grandparents Herb and Leslie Hutchinson honeymooned there shortly after the turn of the 20th Century, but I'm sure it was Herb's parents who first took him to Canandaigua Lake. From the union of Sam Hutchinson (1856) and Mary Ann Finucane (1859) came Herb Hutchinson in 1884; then his youngest daughter, my mother, Ann, in 1924; then me in 1946; then my first daughter Barbara Ann in 1969; and her sons Tyler (2000) and Scotty Davis (2003). Canandaigua Lake: "For as long as we can possibly be, it will be there."

Swimming at Jaeschkes, with cousins Tommy and Janie Dowling, and Steve; Neighborhood football team Jimmie Palmer, Bobbie Cope, the author, Johnny Cufari, Bruce Morgan, Steve in helmet.

Chapter 12

Beyond the Backyards

Uncle Tom Dowling and my father used to crowd us into a car and drive us over on Saturday afternoons to the village of East Rochester, where there was a movie theater. They'd drop us off and pick us up afterward. I didn't know, or even asked, but they probably went down the street to a neighborhood bar while we watched Disney cartoons –- Donald Duck, Goofy, Mickey Mouse -– and a feature film, maybe Disney's "Snow White." It was fun, especially if it was a rainy afternoon.

One time mom and dad took Steve and me and a very young Billy to that theater to watch "Old Yeller." It's the only time I can remember going with my parents to the movies. I was enthralled with the story of the daring yellow dog. In the scene where a wild boar is chasing the boy Travis, I was so into it, I jumped up and started hollering, "Run! Run!" My mother took my hand and said "Jimmy! Shhh!" I sat down, but wasn't even embarrassed because I was so taken away by the story on the screen. Back home, I went next door to the library as soon as I could and took the book out and devoured it.

But mostly we were outside and quite often swimming. Irondequoit Creek in Pittsford was a kid's path to adventure. Whether it was something simple like walking across a fallen tree over the stream while on a hike, or getting out there before 6 a.m. on opening day of trout season, which my brother Steve did every year since I can remember.

One place on the creek was called Jaeschkes (pronounced Jeskies). It was a swimming hole complete with a rope swing and a homemade diving board made out of heavy planks. My father and Uncle Tom Dowling would drive us there. Steve, Billy and I and our cousins, Tommy, Leslie, Janie and Katherine Dowling would crowd into Tom's car. He'd let us ride on the running boards down Eastview Terrace until we got to Jefferson Road. The older Dowlings, Tim and Danny, would be swimming there too, but they'd get there by car with friends.

You'd turn and go down a steep embankment on a dirt road and then drive what seemed to be quite a ways until you got to the bend in the creek we called Jaeschkes, named for the man who owned the last mill near there when grain was loaded onto barges on the canal early in the 20th Century. In the 1950s the mill was gone and Jaeschkes was a swimming hole for the kids of Pittsford. We'd help the adults fill burlap sacks with sand for a homemade dam and repair it each spring, always leaving a little chute for the creek to keep running. But the dam widened the creek into a picturesque swimming playground.

After a while, we'd be so immersed in our own good fun, races across the creek, who could jump the farthest off the rope swing — Tim Dowling could dive off the rope! — we'd barely notice Tom or Dad or any other adults, who were also swimming.

We swam as much as we could. Swimming in Lake Ontario, the easternmost of the Great Lakes, was a true adventure. Lake Ontario was huge; you couldn't see the other side, which was Canada. The lake was pretty much beyond our reach as kids. But Madge ("Auntie") and Lem Lusk had two daughters, Mary Bruce and Betty Griswold, my mother's cousins. In the summers when Mary and her husband Bub took their sons Billy and John to visit Betty and Mack Griswold at their fine home on the shores of Lake Ontario, sometimes it became a family excursion.

Mack and Betty were meticulous. They had perfect flower gardens and a lawn like a golf-course green where we played croquet, carefully. The lawn ended at a 20-foot embankment down to the shore with its amazing smooth and rounded stones, made that way from eons of lapping waves. Lapping may be the wrong word, more like crashing waves; the waves on Lake Ontario could get humongous.

As the adults settled into their lawn chairs and iced teas and mixed drinks, the kids headed for the waves. Inevitably, large tree trunks would float by. We'd swim out, climb on them and paddle closer in to shore. We'd ride the waves and ride the waves. We'd try to stand on the trunks and then we could dive into the cool water. We'd try to ram each other. We wouldn't see an adult until someone's mother came down and hollered that it was time for burgers and hotdogs.

On the other side of my family, my father's side, the Lansing's lived way out "in the sticks" as we'd say, in Ionia, some 15 miles from Pittsford. Dad's sister Rita and her husband Garrett, had a slew of kids. The only one I knew at all was Claire, a year or two younger than me, and a drop-dead gorgeous teen-ager. There was an abandoned quarry way out there with a beautiful, blue-water swimming place that teens would head to on a hot summer Saturday.

Claire would usually be there in a two-piece bathing suit – rare in those days – looking like something out of Playboy magazine. But she was a bit of a tomboy. Sheer cliffs of granite embraced the water. Two in particular were the favored spots for frolicking. One was maybe 12 feet high, the other was more like 20 feet high. My beautiful cousin always dove (not jumped) from the high cliff. And when she got to the edge ready for her dive, every boy there stopped to watch. She was beauty in motion.

Maybe it was remembered scenes like swimming wherever we chose that later conjured up the phrase we hear so often about how those days were "simpler times," partly in the sense that kids could play with abandon wherever and whenever we wanted. But that is too, well, simple. The Cold War didn't make anything simple back in the middle of the 20th Century. There was nothing simple about air raid drills where teachers would instruct us to get under our desks to protect ourselves from hydrogen bombs or nuclear missiles. The teachers would pull the shades. Sometimes we were instructed to go out in the hall, kneel down against the wall and put our hands over our heads. It remains clear to me today that I was thinking then,

"How could this save us?" What I wanted to do was run home and be with Mom; find Steve and get home to protect Mom, who was there with little Billy Smith. There was nothing simple about that.

What does that phrase mean, "simpler times"? We went from lifting the telephone receiver at home and hearing the operator say, "Number, puhlease," and you'd give her a four-digit phone number; to phones with dials on the base where you'd stick your index finger in a hole above each of seven numbers, whirl the dial around to a stopper and let it whirl back to complete a call. No one ever thought of putting a telephone in your pocket and having it with you all the time. Maybe it's simpler to have a phone in your pocket so you can call at any time? But that also means your parents can call at any time.

The Communist takeover of the world was not simple, it was a scary thing for a kid to deal with. Maybe that was part of the magic of not having grownups around. We could leave those ugly thoughts behind. In a very real sense, fun and sports without grownups was part of life in the 1950s, at least in Pittsford — hockey on the canal, baseball, basketball and soccer at Lincoln Avenue School. The men who would coach us in Little League — our one supervised "youth" sport — had played pickup baseball as kids in the 1930s and early '40s on the very spot they later built the Little League field.

We had a neighborhood football team. At first I wore my father's leather helmet from his high school days. Then, somehow, I acquired shoulder pads and a new plastic helmet with a single hard plastic bar that curved across my mouth.

Our neighborhood team included Jimmie Palmer (though he really lived outside the village), Greg Stephany, Bobby Cope, my brother Steve and his friends Bruce Morgan and Johnny Cufari.

We'd ride our bikes down North Main Street, under the railroad underpass, down Washington Road to Topper Connors' big backyard and the Hamptons' field next door. Topper and his brother Jimmy's team included Bob Heffer, Mike Spiegel and Butch MacMillan. By far the best athletes were Mike and Butch and Jimmie Palmer. I'd include Steve Smith, but he was three years younger. Palmer was a natural but Spiegel was a full head taller than all of us. He sprouted early and he could run and jump like an Olympian. Playing against him was a mighty challenge.

It didn't occur to us that we needed adult coaches, umps or refs. Looking back, it was fun and freedom. If there was an off sides, or unnecessary roughness, we'd work it out. There might be arguments, but it was part of the game to resolve disputes. No one looked to a coach about whether to run or pass on the next play.

It was pure exhilaration. Connecting on a forward pass to Jimmie Palmer over Mike Spiegel's head was a sight to behold. We didn't need parents in the stands applauding. The play, the disputes, the games themselves were just us kids. There was no man with a whistle starting a race when we swam in the canal. If a snake came along, you chased it, or not.

As the 1950s became the 1960s, and we had already played for coaches on junior high school teams or Little League, we'd still meet and play ball without an adult in sight.

There was a universal ritual to get the games started called "toss the bat." Usually the acknowledged best players were named opposing captains. One would take a bat – always a wooden bat – and toss it in vertical position, handle at the top, to the other, who caught it with one hand about in the middle of the bat. Then they would go hand over each others' hand to the top of the bat.

Whichever captain's hand fit at the top of the handle, he got first pick of a player; unless the opposing captain could grasp the very top of the bat handle with the tips of his fingers and swing it around his head three times without dropping it. If he did, he got to pick a player first.

Once sides were picked and the game began, the opposing catchers called balls and strikes. If someone slid into second and it was a close play, we'd work it out. These games could go on all afternoon until it was time to go home for supper, or until dark if the game was after supper.

I've often wondered and written newspaper columns about what happens to children when they are constantly supervised by adults, never allowed to go out and just play, never allowed to work out disputes among themselves. What kind of adults will they grow up to be?

In 2010 I came upon a column in The New York Times headlined "On Sandlot Day, Children Call Their Own Shots." It was by Mark Hyman, the author of "Until It Hurts: America's Obsession With Youth Sports and How It Harms Our Kids."

This piece was about a program called Sandlot Day developed by the Youth Sports Institute based at the State University of New York at Cortland. The Institute director, Tim Donovan, was quoted saying: "The lessons learned from choosing up sides — negotiation, conflict resolution — they're the building blocks of civilization."

Sandlot Day was catching on in several communities — just one day, mind you, when the adults would disappear and let the kids play baseball. Then I was surprised to read that the Pittsford, N.Y., Little League liked the idea.

But the organization couldn't leave the kids totally alone, and league leaders planned to have a few parents hanging around.

"The Erie Canal runs by the outfield at two of our fields," said the league president. "I'd like a few adults around so the kids don't jump in."

I didn't know whether to laugh or cry. I guess that guy never had the thrill of jumping off the Main Street bridge into the canal. My first experience with coaches was in Little League. I quickly learned that coaches can be good for a kid, but some coaches should have gone into professional wrestling. Some of them should never have been allowed near kids.

1961 Pittsford JVs (Brighton Pittsford Post). Heading to college on the Erie Canal senior season 1967, (Rochester Times-Union, Bob was from Rochester), the author after a home game.

Chapter 13

Soccer

Recess at St. Louis School, where I went from kindergarten through third grade, was rushing out of the building into the freedom of a parking lot and a small patch of grass. It was a release from the absolute silence enforced in class by the Sisters of Mercy and the requirement to stand up 1) whenever Father Reddington, or any other priest, walked into the classroom; and 2) whenever you were called on to answer a question; and 3) of course, when we prayed.

The best we had at recess was jumpropes, otherwise we ran around playing tag or just running for running's sake. I remember in kindergarten the indignity on that small patch of grass, which was off to the side of the school, of being tackled by Judy Cox and then she climbed on top of me and held me down. Even that young, getting beaten by a girl was, well, not something you wanted to get around. It was good that only a few kids saw it happen. The thing is, she was actually tougher than I was.

Except one night when she and I and my cousins Fran and Janie were in a school play together. The kindergartners made up MacNamara's Band in "An Irishman's Dream" at Town Hall Friday night, March 14, 1952. "At the curtain call," my mother wrote in a scrapbook, "what a surprise to see Jimmy leading the whole band out! He stopped dead in the middle of the stage, and Judy Cox, who wanted to go further but couldn't budge him, finally went around him."

Whew! I'm glad there were no fisticuffs on stage. Judy grew into a cute girl with short, bobbed black hair, but she never got rid of that tomboy reputation.

When I went to public Lincoln Avenue School in the fourth grade on my spiffy new bike, there was a gymnasium, an outdoor basketball court, a tennis court and three baseball diamonds the outfields of which made for a large expanse of green grass.

One of the first kids I met was Butch MacMillan, who lived right across the street from the school. He and I were shooting baskets during a recess in early September when I asked him what all those kids were doing running around and kicking a ball.

He looked at me sort of stunned and said, "They're playing soccer."

"Oh, yeah," I said, and quickly went back to shooting baskets.

When I got home that afternoon I asked, "Hey Mom, what's soccer?"

And so I got my first lesson in the sport that I would play the longest, all the way through college, and then coach two years at the high school varsity level.

We played the sport in school beginning in sixth grade. But I couldn't play my freshman year at Pittsford Central High School because, under state law, at 13, I was too young. Joe Borrosh, the JV coach and my eighth-grade science teacher, who would be an influence on me for years to come, appointed me team manager. I got to carry around the first aid kit and take game movies with a compact film camera that whirred when you turned it on. I think you had to turn a crank every once in a while to keep it filming.

Sophomore year, I made his team and got my picture in the weekly

Brighton-Pittsford Post with Freddie Palmer and Jerry Prudom — the three highest scorers. We were the three centers on the front line. Freddie, who would later play for Dartmouth, was the most agile and most aggressive and scored twice as much as I did. Still, Jerry and I knew how to put the ball in the net, dribbling around defenders and kicking past goalies.

Joe Borrosh knew kids and would go on to become one of the winningest high school varsity soccer coaches in western New York State. In a personal note to me after that JV season he tapped into my intensity and wrote: "Work hard, relax, and your ability will see you through."

He was also one of the best teachers I ever had. I was in his eighth-grade science class his first or second year of teaching. He kept us interested in things I'd never thought I'd care about. He challenged us. He told us one day to go home and propose to our parents that, "If you stop smoking, I promise to never start."

This was four years before the surgeon general's warning that smoking cigarettes "is dangerous to your health." I had to tell him the next day that my parents, who had been smoking two packs a day forever, just stared back at me silently.

As juniors and seniors, Freddie, Jerry and I made the varsity soccer team. Freddie saw considerable playing time. Jerry and I inherited bench positions. Coach Ray Davison hardly ever put me in a game. He did the same thing to me as a sophomore on the JV basketball team. I couldn't get any playing time with him. I wasn't sure why he didn't like me. He barely spoke to me, and then only to scold.

Even when I was a senior he'd rarely put me in a game. My mother walked up to nearly every game but she saw her son play varsity soccer a total of only a few minutes. I felt bad for her that she kept coming, but I felt worse that I hardly ever got out onto the field. Maybe he just thought I wasn't very good at the game.

But Joe Borrosh thought I was good and I came through for him. And then he came through for me. He had played soccer for Brockport State, a legendary soccer powerhouse in the nation, and he wrote a letter of recommendation for me to the college.

"Jim has established an outstanding record . . . demonstrated leadership qualities . . . and a strong desire to succeed," he wrote to Brockport's admissions director. It was the only place I applied, and I was accepted, thanks in part to Mr. Borrosh's trust in me.

Huntley Parker ran the soccer program at Brockport and he welcomed me with a warm letter and invitation to try out. The first year I played on the freshman team. We had an early scrimmage against Monroe Community College and my older cousin Dan Dowling was playing for MCC. Dan, my former algebra tutor, was an individualist. He was somewhere between a highbrow education at the University of Rochester and a tour in Vietnam. I didn't know he was at MCC, much less starting on its soccer team.

As the teams lined up for the game, I was playing right wing and at first I didn't recognize the guy opposite at their left wing. He was the only player on the field wearing black sneakers instead of soccer cleats. When our eyes met I was startled to see Dan smiling back at me.

And I was surprised to see on the sidelines only a few feet away his mother, my mother and Aunt Margaret, whose own son Teddy had been an All American soccer player at the University of Rochester. She exclaimed, way too loudly, "Danny, don't you hurt him!" and pointed at me.

We both laughed, the game began. Dan was a really good ball handler and as scrappy on the field as I was. Opposing wings, forward positions, really had very little to do with each other anyway, and he didn't come close to hurting me.

A few days later, back at Brockport in an inter-squad scrimmage, I'll never forget charging the goal as the ball came flying to the center of the field. It was on a direct line right at me and I had a clear shot at the right corner of the goal. The goalie saw that and dove in that direction. In an instantaneous decision, I let the ball pass by my extended left foot and then, with a quick side action of my trailing right foot, pushed the ball to the left corner of the goal. The goalie was diving one way, the ball went into the net the other way.

Gene Orbacher, an ebullient Scotsman and freshman coach, ran up to me hollering "Laddie! Laddie! Didja mean to do that? Didja mean to DO that?

I nodded, smiled and said, "Yes I did."

My college soccer career had begun.

Next year, as a sophomore, I made the varsity team. It was an elitist feeling. We showed up to school two weeks before everyone else, along with the football team. The campus was ours. When classes began, we got to the dining halls late, but there was always a good meal waiting. Brockport was a soccer school. In fact, the home soccer stands were always more full than the home football stands. Having fellow students cheer you on — cheer for the team, cheer for you — well, it makes you feel blessed on earth.

My first two years I was a reserve right wing (as the position was called back in the 1960s). Before we went home for the summer after junior year, Mr. Parker told me to work out as much as possible kicking with my left foot, because he was pretty sure he was going to start me at left wing senior year.

I got up to the high school kickboard every chance I could that summer of 1967 and kicked with my left foot. With each kick, the ball would bounce back and I'd kick again with my left foot. My closest friend on the team, Bob Champaigne, lived in Rochester. He and I would get together and kick a ball back and forth. I played some soccer, but those summer leagues could get pretty rough and I was saving myself for my senior year at Brockport State.

Bob and I decided to go back to school in style. He had been elected president of the senior class. I had been elected president of the student government. We were two soccer players going back for our last year. We called the Rochester Times-Union and told them we were canoeing from Pittsford all the way to Brockport, 35 miles on the Erie Canal. Being a city kid, Bob had never paddled a canoe. It took us all day and it's a good thing you don't use your hands and arms in the sport of soccer. Champaigne would have been useless. But we got our picture in the paper as we set out for our last year in college.

We chose team captains at the end of the last season. There were paper ballots — you just wrote in the two guys you wanted for co-captains. I wrote in two names. Later, one of the graduating seniors came up to me and said, "You didn't vote for yourself, did you?"

I said no.

"You should have," he said, and told me one of the co-captains beat me out by one vote.

"If you had voted for yourself instead of him, you'd be a co-captain." Lesson learned: Have confidence in yourself.

Bob Champaigne had this easy twinkle in his eyes, always a ready smile and he enjoyed a bit of mischief now and then. He said that the kickboard, just off to the side of the varsity field, looked drab. He suggested the two of us brighten it up.

So we went out and bought some green and gold paint, Brockport's colors. At midnight we painted the whole thing a nice bright green and then painted in gold, "Thou Shalt Not Lose."

It psyched up the team — well, some of the team — and no one ever knew it was Bob and I who did it.

Huntley Parker was a hallowed name. He had won more soccer games in his career than any other coach in the country. He knew the game. He knew kids, but like most coaches, he had his blind spots. Bob was a halfback, a fine defensive player, and the second Champaigne to play for Mr. Parker. But Bob didn't play much. It reminded me of my days on my high school team and I wondered what Bob ever did to Huntley Parker to deserve so much bench sitting.

On the day of our last practice before our last home game, Huntley went down a list and seemed to want to say something about each of the seniors. When he got to Bob, he said that he was incredibly loyal, never missed a day of practice, and supported every player from the sidelines with encouragement during games. Even though Bob has not played, he has been an important member of this team, said the coach.

Bob just sat there and grinned. I was glad Huntley said that, but I wished he had given him more playing time. He did that last game, and Bob played his heart out.

Many of our away games were overnight trips and I mailed a postcard home from whatever motel we stayed at. The final trip was against unbeaten Oneonta State. The postcard was dated Nov. 5, 1967, and addressed to the Smith Family: "Hi — We won 4-2. One assist for the kid, almost one goal. Seems sad this is the last postcard from a soccer game ever. Jim"

We still had our final game at home against New Paltz State. We had two All Americans on the team, Tom Williams and Don Prozik, a Ukrainian-

American with a temper. Don was a big guy, but he had surprising speed and could handle a soccer ball as if he were in a ballet. He played forward. It was my job as a wing to pass the ball in to Don, so he could score. Oh how he scored!

In soccer you never stop moving, so a good pass is always aimed ahead of the player you're passing to. I did that with precision from left wing all season long, and I think I had more assists than anyone on the team. I even scored a few goals from the left side. But mostly it was always pass to Prozik, who would be yelling "Centro! Centro!"

We scrimmaged our last practice. Not real hard, because we were just staying loose for that last game.

Don was yelling "Centro!" at me. I kicked the ball a little late and it landed behind him. He yelled something at me and, well, I sort of short-circuited.

I ran across the field at top speed, wound up and landed my right fist against his face. He fell to the ground with a big thump and I jumped on top of him. I was pummeling him. He was yelling and telling guys to get me off of him.

They did. Huntley came over and said something like "Now boys, let's settle down."

I said to Prozik, "Don't yell 'Centro'! I'll get the ball to you!"

He didn't. I did. Don was about to score the first goal. The goalie blocked his shot, but couldn't hang on to the ball. I was running in from the left and booted it into the net, "an easy shot for Smith," the college newspaper The Stylus reported. Don scored moments later. We won 6-0.

I was about to turn 21. I was 8 years old when I asked my mother what soccer was. She and my father, a high school football star who never really understood soccer, drove to Brockport for nearly every home game my senior year. They saw their oldest son play a lot of soccer. God it was good.

And then Steve came along, a much better player than I was. He made the All Conference team, played a couple of years of professional soccer and then, like Joe Borrosh, became one of the most respected high school soccer coaches in the area.

Last Pittsford varsity game at the Rochester War Memorial 1964 (Brighton-Pittsford Post). My first basketball, shooting baskets in the living room.

Chapter 14

Basketball

My first hoop hung from our living room door. An orange metal arm extended just below the net so when you made a basket and the ball hit that arm, a bell rang. I was surprised my parents got it for me because we were on the second floor right above Great Aunt Una. I was only 5 or 6 years old, but even then I knew to tread lightly and not to disturb Una. So my first basketball exercises were rather genteel.

Not so outside on the Zornows' blacktop driveway where cousin Teddy had a hoop attached to the garage. My brother Steve and I played there endlessly — horse, around the world and one-on-one. We rarely played with Teddy, who was eight years older than I was. But he'd show up every once in a while and dazzle us with jumpers and hook shots.

Winter was a problem and I began to think about the big white barn at the end of our gravel driveway. As kids around the turn of the 20th Century, Auntie and Una had kept horses in it, but the horses were long gone when we were growing up in the 1950s. Una kept her car in the barn. The hayloft upstairs was filled with junk.

We asked our parents if maybe we could convert the upstairs to a basketball court. Dad said he wasn't sure Una would go for that. But one warm summer Saturday in 1958, before I went to seventh grade, he showed up with Uncle Ted's farm truck and backed it up to the barn. Come on, he said, let's make a basketball court.

We pushed old rotting trunks filled with God-knows-what out the upstairs door into that truck. Old broken windows, cracked rough-hewn boards, piles of junk nearly filled the truck. We drove it to the town dump. Then we stopped at the lumberyard and Dad bought a bunch of good pine lumber. He already had a new basket and net.

He pounded a backboard together, attached the basket, and as we held it steady he nailed the backboard to the wall. Then he made a new trapdoor. When closed, it was level with and nearly seamless to the floor.

There were two hazards — metal rods slanted from the floor up to the 6-by-6 uprights midway on each wall, so driving for a layup could be hazardous, and many a visiting player ended up with bruised shins.

The basket was directly below the crest of the roof, which slanted down to the side walls. So playing ball in the barn meant you learned to shoot low from the outside, no arching jumpers. It was bad form but it was basketball, indoors, all winter long.

The final touch was to get the garden hose up there and spray away decades of dust on the floor. A whole lot of boys in the village and beyond at one time or another played basketball in Una's barn.

I went out for the seventh-grade team, as did most of the guys who played in the barn. Mr. Thompson, the coach and a sixth-grade teacher, asked us all during tryouts which was more important, doing your schoolwork or playing on the school team? I could be pretty naïve and answered immediately, making the school team. And, in fact, it was more important to me.

A couple of the kids told me later I shouldn't have said that. Sure enough, Mr. Thompson cut me from the squad. To say that I was devastated doesn't quite explain it. It was a lesson in diplomacy, holding your cards close, not blurting out what you really feel. Mr. Thompson, no doubt, felt

I'd be a better student not being distracted by basketball. He didn't really understand; making the team, playing basketball gave me a feeling of success and made me work harder as both an athlete and a student.

I knew in my heart I was as good as most of the guys who made the seventh-grade team. I swore I was going to make the eighth-grade team. I'd keep my mouth shut about academic priorities, but I'd practice and practice my basketball skills.

I practiced in the barn. I practiced at Zornows'. I went up to Lincoln Avenue School alone and shot baskets for hours at a time on the outdoor court. I still couldn't get the hang of the jump shot. There was this little kick at the top of the jump that I just couldn't master. I'd try it over and over.

Finally, it happened. I figured it out. I did it. I yelled and hollered and jumped around, saying to no one but myself, "I did it! I did it! I can do it!"

Dribble, jump, extend your arms with the ball above your head. At the very top of your jump, kick your feet back, flick your wrists and let the ball go. I shot jumper after jumper until I was sure I had the right rhythm. Then I practiced right-handed and left-handed layups, hook shots and foul shots.

The next December I was selected as the last man on the eighth-grade team. As the season went on I hustled and hustled and by the end of the year I was on the starting five and was voted "most improved player."

Also in eighth grade I won the American History — Good Citizenship Award.

We played our home games at Lincoln Avenue School, which was my mother's high school when, in 1942, she was a varsity cheerleader. There was very little room for a crowd and the basket at one end hung right in front of a big stage. Still, I knew I was playing ball where her varsity used to play.

In the summer when school was out, we used to break in and play in that gym. We couldn't get through the locked doors, but there was a manhole cover just outside the building that led down into the furnace room, which once had a coal furnace. Going through there, coal dust would still cling to your clothes.

Usually Parkie Cowgill volunteered to go down, then come up and open the door into the gym. The county sheriffs inevitably showed up. They'd line us up, ask our names and write them down. We always gave fake names and the cops knew it. They'd scold us and tell us we were breaking and entering, a criminal offense. They also realized it was B&E to play basketball.

I made the freshman team in 1960, the year I was too young to play soccer in the fall. Luckily, the first basketball game was on my 14th birthday, so they let me try out. Some of the freshmen made the junior varsity, but at least I was a starter on the freshman team. Built my confidence. It was a good year.

I made JVs my sophomore year but hardly played. Ray Davison was the coach. Junior year was another disappointment. I didn't make the varsity. After I was cut, I pleaded with Coach Charlie Miller to let me play, to no avail. But he said he needed a seventh-grade basketball coach to work with Mr. Mueller, the eighth-grade coach, and would I be interested? I wasn't, but it was the best I could do and I'd be coaching my brother Steve and Dan Dowling's little brother Tommy. It turned out to be fun and Coach Mueller must have given Charlie Miller good reports. When the varsity team made it to the post-season sectionals, Charlie put me on the team. Just going out onto the high school gym floor in a varsity uniform gave me goose bumps. I didn't get into any games, but it gave me confidence in the tryouts my senior year.

He wrote a note in my junior year yearbook next to the photo of his varsity basketball team: "I want to see you work this summer and be in this picture next year. Coach Miller"

Three seniors I knew endorsed that effort in notes to me in my yearbook. John Alessi, whom I would play soccer with at Brockport State, said, "I don't know when I've met a guy with more desire and hustle as you."

"I expect to hear you're starting on varsity next year," wrote Don Browne. "Keep hustling and you'll make it."

The student council president, a seemingly always smiling Les Loomis, reminded me after I was brought up at the end of the season that "I told you Mr. Miller was fair and that hard work would pay off and it did. Remember that effort seldom goes unrewarded. Next year I expect to see you on the starting five."

Then there was divine intervention. Butch MacMillan transferred out of Pittsford Central to do his senior year at a private prep school. He was the fourth or fifth man on Pittsford's basketball team. His leaving opened a spot on the starting five and I was going for it. The sure starters were Bert Jones, Frank Wakeley, Bill Balden and Dusty Miller. The fifth spot was open and I was going from not making the team my junior year to aiming for that fifth spot.

Then Pete Menihan transferred in from McQuaid Catholic high school. I had played CYO (Catholic Youth Organization) ball with him the previous year. He was 6 feet tall, I was 5 foot, 10 inches. He was smooth with an easy outside jump shot, I was intense and a hustler on the hardcourt. First, of course, we both had to make the team. There were a few juniors with promise, if Coach Miller chose to go that way.

He selected five seniors, including Pete and me. Balden, Jones and Wakeley, the coach's son Dusty Miller, a junior, were all going to start, and deservedly so. The fifth spot was still up for grabs. The headline in the school paper after our first game said it all: "Jones, Smith Pace First Victory." Bert scored 19 points, I had 15 in a 71-36 rout of Honeoye Falls.

Charlie Miller knew how to charge kids up. Once he chose his team he told us we were the New York Yankees of Pittsford. Everyone looked up to the varsity players, he'd say. It was true. The bleachers were always packed. It was as if the whole town showed up for games. It was a night out for the men and women of Pittsford and they roared as loudly as the students in the stands.

Charlie demanded concentration from his players. One day at practice he was pointing out what each guy was doing wrong — he meant this sincerely, not meanly. He wanted each of us to be in top form. Some he wanted to jump more aggressively for rebounds. Others he wanted better concentration and knowing where the ball is. To me, he yelled, "And Jimmy, get the stardust out of your eyes!" We all knew what he meant.

The vivacious and pretty blonde Sue Hastings had been my steady girlfriend for more than a year. We walked the halls together between classes, lingered at our lockers and went out together every weekend. To Charlie Miller, basketball came first and girlfriends were a distraction. But that weekend Sue and I went to Seabreeze Amusement Park in nearby

Irondequoit. At one of the booths — it must have been the basketball hoops — I won her a big stuffed dog. We named it Stardust.

The parents of players all sat together, a coterie of support. The school principal, Arnie Carlson, always welcomed them. It must have been particularly special to him and my mother. He played on the 1941-42 Pittsford varsity basketball team when she was a cheerleader. I wondered if she cheered for him the way my cousin Janie Dowling cheered for me. Before each game the cheerleaders, in their tight white sweaters and blue skirts, led the crowd in a cheer for each player. Janie and I had been in school together since kindergarten. We were nearly sister and brother. During warm-ups I'd watch her out of the corner of my eye. She cupped her hands to her face and yelled: "Smith!" Then she'd jump and yell "Smith! Jim Smith! Yeah bo Jim Smith!" as the crowd chanted with her. Her next-door neighbor Patti Bridge did the cheer for Bert. They did that for each player. What a truly amazing feeling.

I was usually one of the smaller players in the game — 5' 10" and 145 pounds. Early in the season, we were playing rival Fairport at home. Both Pete Menihan and I were in the game. Pete went up for a layup when Fairport's Sammy Stolt, their star football player with no basketball grace, decided to just kind of barrel into Pete, who fell to the floor. I ran in from behind and pushed my chest up against the much larger Stolt. Standing just off to the side was Principal Arnie Carlson, laughing at the sight of me facing off with Stolt. But in came Bert Jones, our gentle giant who could be ferocious. He stepped between me and Stolt and then Arnie wasn't smiling, he was getting worried. Bert didn't budge. It was Stolt who backed away as the ref rushed over.

Bert had been playing on the varsity since his sophomore year. He and I weren't close friends. He was more a part of the in-crowd. But we were good together on the court. He liked to have my hustle and my defense in the game. And I had a ton of assists passing to Bert for the shot. Mid-season, Pete Menihan had edged me out as a starter for a couple of games in a row. Then in the next pre-game psyche talk Mr. Miller announced the starting five and I was back in. Last thing in the locker room before a game was always the team handshake. We'd move in close, join our hands and yell

"Go Knights!" This time as we untangled I couldn't pull my right hand out. Another hand was holding tight. I looked up and there was Bert with a big grin. He was glad I was back in. That silent gesture meant a lot to me and I played harder that game than ever.

Only one thing truly interrupted my varsity basketball reverie that senior year of 1963-64. We were sitting in history class just after lunch on Friday, Nov. 22, when Mr. Carlson announced over the PA system that President Kennedy had been shot. I looked right at our teacher, Mr. Kreiser, a tough old man, and he was stunned, he had fear in his eyes. The principal didn't say if the president was dead or alive, only that there would be more information. Class ended a few minutes later. Out in the hall, Sue rushed up to me, crying, "Is he dead? Is he dead?"

No one knew. We must have gone to final homeroom like every day, but as the last bell rang I rushed to her room, we ran out to the parking lot and turned on my car radio. There we learned that President Kennedy was dead. We held each other. There were knots of students at a lot of cars with radios on. I told her I'd take her home, but first I went to the gym, almost wanting to have basketball practice. I knew we wouldn't. How could we? Mr. Miller told us our game was cancelled that night.

Driving my girlfriend home, I turned the corner onto Elmwood Avenue, her street, and there was a man raking leaves on his lawn. "He probably doesn't even know the president is dead," I said to her.

When I got to 25 North Main Street my mother's face was solemn as she sat in front of the TV. As a family we watched it all weekend, the swearing-in of Lyndon Johnson on Air Force One as Jackie Kennedy stood next to him with blood on her dress. The funeral cortege — we learned a new word: cortege. History class, high school, even varsity basketball seemed very small and far away.

My cousin Katie Kinsky was an editor of our senior yearbook, "Highlights '64." In the front they put a photo of the high school flag at half-mast. The facing page had some words from John F. Kennedy's undelivered speech in Dallas:

"We in this country, in this generation, are — by destiny rather than choice — the watchmen on the walls of world freedom. We ask, therefore, that we may be worthy of our power and responsibility — that we may exercise our strength with wisdom and restraint."

He had been so young. He had little children in the White House and a beautiful young wife. My friends and I were coming of age in a sense of feeling empowered and independent as he and Jackie were ascending to the leadership of our country. We had new music, we had a new generation, we had a new young president and then he was cut down.

Monday we went back to school. I wasn't ready to learn. We were all kind of going through the motions. At basketball practice that afternoon, I began to pick it up. I began to say to myself that we all need to try harder because JFK is not around anymore. We all did what we could — we remembered we were a team and we had some victories to earn.

It was Pittsford's first year in the AA league with the bigger high schools in the county and we were not expected to make the postseason tournament. In fact, it came down to one playoff game between us and Fairport to decide which team would go on to a chance to play in the Rochester War Memorial, our Madison Square Garden.

We played at a neutral site. The place was packed to the rafters. It was a low-scoring, intense game. Fairport was coming down the court with the ball. I chased the guy, who dribbled over the centerline, reached in and cleanly swatted the ball away. I dashed for it and headed back down toward our basket. The crowd was roaring. I was alone, the basket inviting me. I raced, dribbling through the din of the excited crowd, then somehow my feet were wrong for my natural right-handed layup, so at the last second I shifted, laid it up lefty and a Fairport player slashed past me. I could see the ball loop around the rim, then I fell to my knees. I heard a collective groan from the bleachers. The ball fell out and Fairport grabbed the rebound. There was no time to lick wounds or even for regrets. I rushed back up the court and crouched in defense again, anguished at missing an easy shot, but intent on staying in the game. I still have dreams, decades later, about that play and the ball rolling around the rim and out.

At halftime we led 21-19. Charlie Miller was anything but calm in the locker room. "What's wrong with you guys! The only one hustling out there is Jimmy! But Jimmy, why did you lay that up with your left hand?"

That's all I remember him saying. Neither team exactly roared back in the second half. But in the end, Pete Menihan cemented it for us with a foul shot. With nine seconds remaining, Pete put us up 40-37 and that's how the game ended. Bert, Dusty Miller and Frank Wakeley, all in double figures, had 35 of those 40 points.

We were on to the sectionals. In the first game we edged out Batavia 60-59 when Bert grabbed a rebound and hung on to it as the clock ticked the final seconds away. We were on to the quarter-finals against powerhouse Eastridge in the War Memorial on March 14, 1964. There were three games that day, with the smaller high schools playing first. Pittsford v. Eastridge was the headliner that night. Our crowds at home of a couple thousand fans burgeoned to upwards of 7,500 at this altar to upstate New York sports extravaganzas.

Eastridge High from Irondequoit, a northern suburb of the city, had the highest scorer in the league, 6 foot, 2 inch Sam Adamo, who averaged well over 20 points a game. Coach Miller decided on a "box and one" game strategy. He was pulling one player to do nothing but shadow Adamo. That player would be me, 5 foot, 10 inch me. I was even to go to the Eastridge huddles at timeouts, or as close to them as I could get. The moment the teams broke back for the game, I was to be at Adamo's side, never leaving it. With a couple of breathers when Pete came in to relieve me, the strategy worked. Adamo scored one basket the entire game, and six free throws for a total of eight points.

The trouble was our offense. Pete and I were essentially out of the offense. That left four against five defenders. Frank Wakeley was on fire. He scored 18 points. But nobody else scored double figures. We lost the game 50-46. I was devastated.

It seemed like a long way to the locker room. I didn't think it would be our last game. I sat down on a bench and put my head in my hands. Then I began untying my sneakers. Then tears came. Silent tears. Varsity basketball players don't cry. But I was.

Frank looked at me and said, "What's the matter?"

"It's over," I said. "It's over."

Dick Alderman was a soccer teammate of mine and the president of our senior class. He wrote in my yearbook, "You showed me if you want something bad enough and work for it, you'll get it, of course you know I'm talking about basketball."

On the starting five, I was the only one under 6 feet and the only one not to make All County. Bert, Frank, Dusty and Bill were all named to the All County team. Bert had been playing varsity for three years. He had this reputation of being a big tough jock, which he was. But ever since that locker room handshake and his big smile, I saw him differently. I can't remember what I wrote in his yearbook, but he wrote in mine, "You were really a pleasant surprise in basketball this year, you helped us win many games."

Our final season in high school was baseball. Bert and I and Charlie Hanner would be elected co-captains, but no one would have any reason to say I helped the team.

Little League 1959

Chapter 15

Baseball

As the snow melted each spring we found the first patch of green grass for tossing a baseball, always at the corner of our barn off to the side of the driveway leading into the library lawn next door. I pulled my glove out from under the bed where it had been all winter, tied and folded over a hardball. I'd spit in the pocket and swirl it all around, loosen up the leather and head for that patch of grass, throwing the ball back and forth with Greg Stephany as March turned to April.

The big Rochester AM radio station, WHAM, carried Yankees games. Nearby Syracuse was the home of their Triple A farm club, so it was natural in upstate New York to grow up a Yankees fan. The Rochester Red Wings were the Cardinals' farm team in the 1950s, so my favorite National League team was St. Louis, with Stan Musial and Red Schoendeinst and a guy named Wally Moon.

But I worshipped Mickey and Yogi and Whitey and Moose. My family got a puppy from the pound and we named him Yogi. We hoarded Yankees baseball cards, checked their stats in the paper and hoped the Mick would beat Roger Maris in pursuit of Ruth's homerun record. I reached back to Lou Gehrig after finding a biography about him in the library next door. There was a scene of how he wounded a bird with his BB gun and felt so bad he never shot it again. I was amazed when I read that, because I did the exact same thing and gave up BB guns. I read everything I could find on him — the Iron Horse of major league baseball, never missed a game until that terrible disease got him, the disease they named after him.

I wanted to get to Cooperstown and the Baseball Hall of Fame just to see Lou's uniform hanging in his locker with his glove and his spikes. I pestered my parents about going. Finally my father said OK.

It was 1959, Andy was just born, so he and Mom were staying home. But Bill, Steve and I were going with Dad to Cooperstown in his 1956 green and white Ford Fairlane. It was too far for a day trip so we were going to stay overnight in a motel. A real trip — we were going on a real trip with Dad — to the Baseball Hall of Fame.

We were chattering the whole way. Billy was only 5, Steve was 10, I was 12, at the top of my game my last year in Little League. In fact, I would make the All Star team.

We were cruising with Dad down the New York State Thruway, then onto country roads heading southeast to Cooperstown. Dad said we were almost there. Just over this big hill up ahead was the village that housed the Hall of Fame, he told us — and then the car stalled.

He glided over to the side of the road. He got out and lifted the hood. He got back in and turned the key. The car started again. He moved it into drive and we slowly started up that hill but the car stalled again.

I was getting really upset. We were almost there! "Dad, we gotta get there!"

"I know it, Jimmy," he said.

He got the car started again, but it wouldn't move when he put it in gear. I started crying, but made myself stop. Then he discovered that the car moved in reverse.

He somehow turned it around and we went up that hill backwards! When we got to the top, he turned it around again and we coasted down the hill and right into a gas station in Cooperstown.

Dad talked to a mechanic, then we got our suitcase and we walked to a motel. We found a diner, ate burgers and fries, then Dad walked us back to the motel. He turned on the TV and there was boxing on. He told us to watch the fights and to keep our eye on Billy. And off he went.

We'd never been in a motel before. Watching turned into raging pillow fights and wrestling all over that room with its two beds. At one point Steve said, "Hey, where's Billy?"

He was gone. It was dark. We ran outside and soon found him on a swing set, all alone. We got him back inside, and by the time Dad got back, the three brothers were asleep in one bed.

In the morning I could hardly wait to get to the Hall of Fame. The first thing we saw was this huge bat the size of a telephone pole over the entrance. Inside, as soon as I could, I found Lou Gehrig's locker. I just gazed and gazed at Number 4. His first baseman's mitt was ridiculous, I thought. How could anyone catch a ball with that little thing? What guts and talent the players of Lou's generation had. And Lou never missed a game.

That's really all I needed to see. Even Ruth's display was secondary to Gehrig's in my mind, and Dad wasn't one for hanging around. In fact, I heard him say to one guy, "Boy, this place is boring."

We stopped at the garage and checked on the car. Then we got on a Greyhound bus. I heard the driver say that no, he couldn't stop on the Thruway, we'd have to go all the way to Rochester. But Dad worked something out because during that long ride the bus pulled over and we got off. We climbed up the embankment and found ourselves on Route 31 outside of Pittsford. A guy dad knew came along, picked us up and dropped us off at 25 North Main Street.

Tom Dowling owned the Gulf station in town then. Dad told him the Cooperstown garage would replace the transmission (or was it the engine?) for something like $800. Tom said he'd find a used one, and he did for about $200. He and dad drove back to Cooperstown to tow the 1956 Ford back to Tom's station.

The way Tom told it, they were cruising along the Thruway when my father started honking the horn. Tom pulled over to the side, walked back to

Dad, who said, "The Vernon exit is just up here. Let's go to Vernon Downs for a couple of races."

"Are you crazy?" responded Tom. He got back in his car and continued the tow back to Pittsford.

It was an expensive trip for my father. In fact, it was the last time we ever went anywhere.

But there was Little League in the summer. I was on the Lions. Steck Matthews was the coach. Dad helped coach the Firemen with Rip Palmer, his son Jimmie's team. I don't think any of us kids thought deeply about Little League coaches. I never thought about how those guys, when they were kids, played baseball together before there was Little League.

One place they played was the very spot where, years later, they built our Little League field. Beyond our wooden green outfield fence was the canal. When Dad was a kid, he later told me, they used to have contests on who could hit a ball into the canal. He could. I'm not sure how they got their baseballs back, but they must have. No one was afraid of diving into the canal.

He also told me that Rip Palmer challenged him to a race; the winner got a great prize — the tall, beautiful, leggy Ann Hutchinson with the long dark hair framing her pretty face and easy smile. Rip insisted they run barefoot, out to the canal and back. Rip was speedy, but my father won the race. "Hutch" would hardly allow herself to be the prize for a barefoot race, but a few years later she married my father.

Those guys, those Little League coaches — when they were kids — had also played baseball behind what was then the high school on Lincoln Avenue. This was before World War II, before they went off to fight. This was the summers of 1939, '40 and '41 — the year of DiMaggio's 56-game hitting streak; the year Williams hit .406.

When our time came, we played there too. Home plate was in exactly the same spot. What I didn't know when I was a kid was that my father once hit a pitch over the school and out onto Lincoln Avenue. One day, just a few years ago on a trip home, I drove to the old school, which had become a senior center. I walked to the back corner of the property where home plate used to be and I counted off the distance to the school, over it and out to the street. Five hundred feet. My father hit that pitch seven decades ago, five hundred feet. Incredible. Had I known that as a kid, I think I would have tried harder to be a better hitter. I was a pretty near flawless fielder and a brazen catcher, but I sure was no power hitter. When we had pickup games behind Lincoln Avenue School, I was generally picked in the middle of the pack; not last, but not first either.

I'd go down to Jimmie Palmer's house, a little ranch in one of Pittsford's first housing developments outside the village, and we'd play catch. We both had catcher's mitts and we'd throw fastballs at each other. Jimmie was a better player than I was. He could line homeruns over the Little League fence. Once I bounced one over for a ground rule double, but I never hit a homerun.

To get to a game, I'd push my mitt onto the handlebars of my 24-inch Huffy Western Flyer bicycle, pedal up North Main Street, down State Street, a right on Boughton Avenue with its tall chestnut trees and cement sidewalks ("step on a crack, you'll break your mother's back!") in front of the little houses, a left on Austin Park dead-ending at the dirt path along the canal to the Little League field. My Aunt Jane Dowling ran the food stand. You could get a hotdog for a quarter, a bottle of Coke for a dime and a Three Musketeers bar for a nickel.

I loved being a catcher. I loved calling the pitches, crouching in the dirt and dust, calling plays. I remember one game Tommy Hicks was pitching, Ray Wallman was at shortstop, Greg Stephany at second base and Chuck Cunningham at first. I went out to the mound and pulled the infielders in for a quick conference. There were runners on first and third.

"Look you guys, that guy on first is going to try to steal second and if I throw to second, the runner at third will come in to score," I told the huddle. "So let's do this: I'm going to make a big show of throwing to Greg at second, but Wally, you come running in and I'm going to zip the ball to you. Then you zing it right back to me and we'll get the runner trying to come home."

Wally had a big grin. He loved strategy. Everyone agreed to the play. Tommy pitched, I feigned to second, threw to Wally charging in from shortstop, he lined it back to me and I tagged the guy coming home. That was part of being the catcher and I cherished it.

I made the 1959 Pittsford Little League All-Star team as the second-string catcher. Jimmie Palmer was the first-string catcher. Then he got poison ivy all over his arms and he couldn't handle all that gear so the All-Star coach moved him to the outfield. He still wanted Jimmie's bat in the lineup. I was so ready to get into an All-Star game, but instead the coach put Sam King — who still had another year to play — behind the plate. We were eliminated after two or three games and I never played, not even one at-bat. Leaving the field after that last game with my head down, I tried to hold tears back, but they flowed. Norm Hicks, Tommy's father, saw me and said, "Hey, Jimmy, c'mon. There's next year."

"No, Mr. Hicks. This is my last year," I said. He just looked sad.

That's how my Little League career ended. But it wasn't the end of baseball. I played catcher from age 7 to age 17. As a junior on the high school varsity team, I was, again, the second-string catcher. Bert Jones was first string. When the coach wanted him to pitch, I'd go in and catch. One game against Rush-Henrietta, I replaced Bert behind the plate. His first pitch was a fastball, low, and the batter hit it straight up, about a mile high. It drifted over toward the backstop, then back toward the plate. I kept my eye on it and caught it for the out. I was surprised to hear the umpire say, "Nice catch."

I managed to mumble a "thank you," and thought what a schmuck I'd have been if I'd missed it. Bert could throw heat, as they say; and so could two other across-town Allen Creekers playing varsity baseball for Pittsford Central — Gary Arnold and Dick Kladstrup. It made you wonder if there wasn't something in the water in Allen's Creek.

Two outfielders, incredibly different boys from Pitttsford, had the same rifle arms. Our center fielder, Bill Bolin, was the most unassuming guy, always smiling, always friendly to everyone, always ready to help with anything. Same with Mike McEwen in left field, except that kid was wound as tight as the seams on a baseball. Both could catch a fly running back deep, take one step forward and peg a hardball to me at the plate, and it would be a strike. They could nail a guy trying to get home from third.

Bill, Charlie Hanner, John "Lefty" Dalton and I were a loose foursome of sorts, hanging out together, double dating and playing sports, except for Lefty. He once struck out in a gym class softball game. I wrote it up, mimicking "Casey at the Bat" for the high school newspaper as a practical joke — my first published piece. But I ended up feeling badly about it. When Lefty struck out in softball in front of the entire school, well, I think he never forgave me for that. He loved sports, but he never quite made the final cut to make the teams. As an adult, he would teach and coach for decades.

Our senior year at Pittsford Central, I was elected co-captain with Bert and Charlie, both superb ballplayers who attracted professional scouts to some of our games. I could play the game, but the scouts weren't there to see me. And apparently our coach didn't think much of my playing skills that year.

One day early in the season I was walking out to the field carrying catcher's gear with Coach Bill DiPaulo. I had it in my head I might get more playing time if I said to him I'd like to try third base as well as catching. He just sort of looked at me funny and didn't say anything. I don't know what I ever did to him, but he never let me play that whole year, not catcher, not third base. When we made it to the sectionals and were playing at Rochester Red Wing Stadium, instead of sitting the bench, each inning I got to be the first-base coach. A whole season of never catching, not even one pitch, not one at-bat.

Near graduation at the spring sports awards dinner, team captains always went up to the lectern to get all the players' letters from the coach. Bert and Charlie and I went up and he handed letters to them, shook their hands. When it was my turn, he was out of letters, didn't shake my hand, and uttered something under his breath like "ugh."

I walked back to the baseball team table with a heavy heart, wondering what was wrong with that man.

Sue Hastings, Carol Nobles, Ann Villnow, Barb Moore

Chapter 16

Girls

There was the day in fourth grade that Mrs. Brown told the whole class how I was sweet on the really cute Bonnie Butler. "Do you like a certain blonde in the room, Jimmy?" she teased as Bonnie and I sat there red-faced. But my first real true love was the ever-elusive Carol Nobles. The summer of 1959 heading into eighth grade I fell hopelessly for the cute, shy, petite redhead. We were born just one day apart, yet she was not, and I was, a very young 12-year-old.

She knew I was smitten and I hoped beyond hope that she was too. There was a big problem, however. Whenever I saw her I got all goosey inside, but had absolutely no clue how to act on my feelings. I knew what a kiss was and I longed to kiss her lips, but beyond that, well, it was all a mystery to me.

My pretty 16-year-old cousin Betsy Zornow, who lived next door, was dating Carol's brother Ronnie. Somehow I was invited one Saturday night to go with Betsy to their house. I was so excited I could barely breathe.

More than half a century later, I hold two images from that night. The first is Carol and I outside, sneaking around the bushes and peeking in the window at Ronnie and Betsy making out on the living room couch. Carol would giggle and pull me away from the window — pulling being the important part; in other words, she touched me.

Then there was the walk home. It was only a few blocks. Ronnie and

Betsy were holding hands. Carol and I walked a ways behind them. The streetlights glowed through the dark as we passed under the tall trees of Pittsford's village. If they could hold hands, I thought, so can we, but I didn't dare ask. So I inched my hand toward Carol's and my hand brushed hers. I looked at her. She looked back silently with a smile. I was sure she would have let me take her hand, but I didn't dare. I could throw from a crouch behind home plate and nail a kid trying to steal second, but I couldn't make my hand take hers.

We walked without talking. I kept thinking what a chicken I was, and then we were at North Main Street way too soon. Betsy kissed Ronnie good night. Maybe Carol would have let me kiss her, but I never found out. And before I knew it, she and her brother were walking back to their house. I stood and watched them until they turned the corner and were gone.

I wrote about her nearly 20 years later in a July 24, 1977, story in the Rochester Democrat & Chronicle's Upstate Sunday magazine. It was titled "J.S. + C.N." and was published after the village had turned the library lawn into a parking lot.

I wrote how I grew up next door and how the library lawn had a few trees, including a big one with two trunks that helped support a wobbly old wire fence held up by metal rods. Carol had "red hair and dimples and looked great in a pair of shorts . . . just waiting for her at the corner to walk with her to school made my heart beat faster."

The story explained that I was young, "still climbing trees and carrying my jackknife. The first limb large enough to sit on in that double-trunked tree next to the old fence was about 12 feet from the ground — it could keep my secret.

"Perched there, I pulled the jackknife from my pocket and carefully — not because I was afraid of falling, but because I wanted it done just right — I carved our initials:

J.S. + C.N.

"Every once in a while during those few months of first love, I climbed back up there just to look at the initials. Caught up more in my own private thoughts and less in paying attention to where I was, I fell from that limb. My arm hit one of the metal fence rods and the scar on my inside right elbow is still there."

As I've said, the library lawn was part of our playground, where we played everything from hide and seek to football games. But when it was gone, when they paved paradise, as Joni Mitchell sang, what hit me in the gut was that the tree with our carved initials was gone. I hadn't seen Carol since we graduated from high school in 1964, but she had read the story in Upstate, got my address from my mother and sent me a thank-you note.

That sent me back to the high school yearbook, where I found this from her, written in fine script three years after my unfulfilled romance:

"Jim, I'm not very good at words so you probably won't understand what I'm saying. I guess I really don't know myself either. I will never forget good ole' junior high."

She continued on about how we hadn't seen much of each other since then and when we finally did, "I was really happy to see that you haven't changed a bit." Then she said it was "much too long" to stay apart and agreed how "we have a unique understanding & friendship. Let's hope we always keep it — Always, Carol."

Ain't it funny the way things go. Maybe long distance, over the decades, she and I are "always." What a fine thought.

But there I was in ninth grade and no red-headed girlfriend. So I asked one of her friends, Pam Coerse, to a school dance. We ended up dancing "cheek-to-cheek," embracing each other as we swayed to slow songs like "I Love How I Love You" by the Paris Sisters. Mr. Costello, the assistant principal, would stroll by and tell us the rule was only one arm around each other while dancing. This might have been the night of the twist contest to Chubby Checker. We took second place.

A little later in the year at a freshman party at someone's house, I found myself necking on a rec-room couch with Patty Stell, another of Carol's friends. I was, for the first time, in la-la land. All of a sudden, she bolted upstairs. I could hear her say, "He says he loves me!"

Then, hurried responses: "Wow, he said that!" "Get back down there!" "Just don't let him. . ."

Don't let me do what? I thought. I didn't know any moves at all. Most of the guys I knew had older brothers who told them everything. They knew it. Not me; I was the oldest brother and nobody, including my parents, ever clued me in.

One day in gym class while we were getting dressed in the locker room I asked Dick Kladstrup, whom I had gotten to know as a friend, how you, um, did it. He howled and started hollering, "Hey, Jimmy doesn't know how to do it!"

When the whole locker room full of freshmen boys stopped laughing and taunting, Dick leaned over and not very quietly exclaimed something like how girls have a place right between their legs — "In front! Try it sometime!"

I was pretty sure Dick had never tried it. Maybe his older brother who was a senior had done it, but not Dick. After I was done being embarrassed, I decided never to confide in Dick Kladstrup again.

I don't know if it got around that I was now, at 13, educated in the ways of love, but girls started inviting me to meet them where they were babysitting. Ingrid Thompson invited me to her house because her parents were away. She was tall, statuesque, with long, light brown hair. But she had a dress on with a blouse under it. We were on her living-room couch and about all I was doing was fumbling around. Then the doorbell rang. It was 11:30 p.m. and my father was there to pick me up. Ingrid didn't invite me back.

Then Donna Carson asked me to meet her where she was babysitting, but to be sure to arrive only after the parents had left. I did. Her charges were asleep. We got as far as taking our sneakers off and kissing on the couch. Then we heard a car door slam and the front door open. They were home early. I grabbed my sneakers and ran out the back door. I called her the next day and she told me, "I'm going out with R.J. now." R.J. was a worldly upperclassman.

"Oh, OK," I said.

I think it was the beginning of sophomore year when the exquisite blonde Ann Villnow, a very pretty and quiet girl, asked me to babysit with her. She told me where and when. It was walkable. No father arriving to pick me up. When I got there, she gently pulled me onto the couch and we made out for a long, sweet time. I had no idea such a quiet girl could entwine and whisper lovely things in what seemed perfect harmony. Though only our sneakers actually came off, it was pure blissful dishevelment.

We managed to stop before the parents came home. I leisurely put my sneakers back on. We stood up, hugged and nudged into one more lingering kiss.

I don't remember one shred of conversation that night, but I was amazed by her. I thought she was a very, very special girl. Yet I told myself, thought about it for the next few days, wondered about it — that I didn't really have what I fathomed back then as girlfriend/boyfriend feelings for her. And I thought it would be wrong to keep meeting. And that's what I told her. She didn't talk to me for a long time. She was into the arts clubs. I was basically a jock, or trying to be. We were not — what was I thinking — on the same wavelength? In the same crowd? And, two years out, I was still pining for Carol Nobles. Yet it nagged at me that Ann was someone apart who deserved the best and she certainly deserved honesty. In our senior year I still felt a little guilty about "dropping" her, and must have said something because she set me straight, writing in my yearbook:

"I'm afraid you have a very wrong idea. I don't know of a greater guy in our school. Sincerity and individuality are unusual around here, but you stood out and always will because you have both. I wish you the most important thing in life — happiness always."

Ann was voted "Most Artistic," "Best Dressed" and "Has Done Most for the Class" of 1964. She was one classy girl.

And she had a point. High school isn't a great place for individuality. Just about everyone is trying to be popular in one in-crowd or another. And sincerity, she was right, wasn't exactly a prized value at Pittsford Central High School. I don't suppose that being sincere was at the top of many teenagers' list of proper behavior. Ann Villnow is the one who stood out.

And Barb Moore. That twist contest very well might have been with Barb, who created quite a stir among the high school boys when she came to Pittsford Central our freshman year. She was both cute and beautiful and she agreed to go to a school dance with me. Then she pretty much ignored me all night. It seems to me now that I found her for the contest and we twisted to second place.

She was an "Allen Creeker," kids who came to Pittsford from Allen Creek School, which had been in the next-door Brighton school district. For some reason they started to come to PCS. They were kind of glamorous:

Barb, Patsy Joyce, Bert Jones, Dick Kladstrup — hotshots, instantly popular.

I was amazed Barb agreed to go to a dance with me. We never dated again, though we remained friends throughout high school. In fact, I spent a lot of time our senior year advising her on how to handle her new boyfriend, Charlie Hanner, co-captain of the baseball team. What did I know? I'd say to myself, if she were my girlfriend I'd just worship her all day and all night. Well, if Barb sought my advice, I'd listen and then give as much "advice" as I could. It meant spending time with her and I was grateful for the chance.

"We did have some pretty good talks," she wrote in my yearbook, "What a loss my high school years would have been without you." Alas, she was Charlie's.

Besides, it was another Allen Creeker who took over my life. Sue Hastings arrived in high school in tight sweaters and short skirts, skirts above the knees. In 1961 no one had yet heard of miniskirts, but this petite, pretty, sexy blonde was leading the way there.

I crashed her 15th birthday party. She lived in a huge stucco house on tony Elmwood Avenue in Brighton. I wandered around to the back. I found it odd that a mansion had a rope swing hanging from a giant tree near the screened-in, two-story back porch. Sue's backyard sloped steeply down so that when you swung out, you were really high off the ground. That's where I met her, at that swing.

I wasn't an invited guest, but my cousin, Martha Kinsky, was, and she introduced us. Sue got on the swing and asked me to push her — out she went, over her backyard. Then she gave me a turn. Best swing I'd ever been on. Then we stood and talked, but soon some kids came out looking for her and she went back inside with them. I went home.

When we met in the hall in school Monday she called me Bill. I told her I was Jim and asked her out that Saturday. She said OK. We double-dated with Lefty Dalton, who had his driver's license. I was still 15, too young to drive. I don't remember where we went except to Don & Bob's, a burger joint. But I remember the back seat of the car and her short skirt and how she lay right across me and kissed me with her young, luscious, full lips. We clung to each other. Talk about entwined — holy cow!

The date was Oct. 11, 1962. It ended after midnight, Oct. 12. She was a sophomore, I was a junior. Johnny Mathis's hit "The Twelfth of Never" on Columbia Records became our song — "You ask how long I'll love you/ I'll tell you true/ Until the twelfth of never/ I'll still be loving you."

Three days later came the Cuban Missile Crisis, where for 13 days President John F. Kennedy stared down Nikita Khrushchev of the Soviet Union, who was sending missiles by ship to Cuba. There was a palpable feeling that the Twelfth of Never might come sooner than later. It was not a time for young love to blossom. It was days and nights of worrying about oblivion. Kennedy set up a blockade, essentially daring Russia to try and run it. In the end the Soviet Union blinked and JFK became the world's hero, our hero. Yet, teenagers get absorbed in themselves easily and we were right back in our own little world.

I graduated in June 1964. Sue and I never dated anyone else that whole time; well, just once each, my senior year. Basically, beginning with that first date when, for the first time, I dared to stroke a lovely bare thigh under that short skirt, we were inseparable.

It was called "going steady," an understatement for Sue and me. We met after nearly every class and walked the three minutes together to our next class. We went out nearly every weekend. We snuck into the library next door (I was still stacking firewood in the community room and had a key) and made out for hours on a big soft couch. One night the janitor arrived and we jumped out a window. As he ran out the front door, we were calmly walking down the sidewalk.

"Did you see anybody run by here!" he exclaimed.

"Nope," we could honestly reply, but I was walking without any shoes. And I needed those shoes, so I admitted it was us and could I go in and get my shoes.

The guy was angry and warned, "What if I had a gun? I thought it was a robber. What if I shot at you?"

But we promised not to do it again and he let me get my shoes. And we were undeterred. The library at 21 North Main Street — where my mother was born, where I had mowed the lawn for $2 on Saturday mornings, where my "Auntie" was the librarian and her sister, Una, was a founder of Pittsford Community Library — became our love nest on Saturday nights.

Oh, we'd go to lots of the big parties held mostly in the new developments when someone's parents weren't home. We'd double-date to the drive-in. We went to all the school dances, she came to all my games. But a whole lot of time it was just Sue and me, wherever we could find a spot.

One spot was my new car, my first car. Just as I meant to ride to school in fourth grade on a grand new bicycle, I was tired of walking to the high school and that summer before senior year I told my parents I needed a car. I had been working full-time summers since freshman year and I had a little saved. One night my father came home from work and said he thinks he found a good car for me over in Fairport. He had worked at the Fairport Herald weekly newspaper and knew the car dealership manager.

"I've seen the car," he said, "You'll like it and you'll like the price." It was 1963 and you could buy a new car for about $2,500. "It's a Plymouth convertible, black. That was the only color for cars made in 1948," he said.

"1948? How much, Dad?" I asked.

"A hundred and forty bucks. It's got over a hundred thousand miles, but it's in good condition." He'd take me over that Saturday.

When I saw it, I loved it. I'd have the coolest car in town, I thought. I'd taken $140 out of my savings account, but the dealer found a cracked head gasket and fixed it for $12.50. All I had was the $140. I thought the dealership should include the repair price in the sale price, but it didn't think so. Either did Dad. He pitched in the $12.50. I was heading to school my senior year in style.

Every guy wanted to see it, get in it, drive it. But only I was driving this baby. I'd put the top down, crank up the radio, especially when "Wipe Out" by the Surfaris came on. I'd put 2 bucks' worth of gas in, cruise around Pittsford, pick up my girlfriend in Brighton, and cruise with her sitting right at my side, touching.

My father's friend, my Uncle Tom Dowling, also loved my new car. He must have checked with Una because one day he drove into our driveway with a pickup truck load of gravel. Una's car was on the right side of the barn, the left side had a dirt floor and my father never used it for his car.

"C'mon, Jimmy, grab some shovels," Tom exclaimed. Presto, a floor for my "Plymmy." I thought that was real thoughtful of my Uncle Tom.

The Plymmy's most glorious moment was with Tom's oldest son, Tim Dowling. He and I worked together at Monroe Golf Club. Sometimes I'd drive him home from work, heading through the village. One Saturday afternoon we ran into the annual parade for the opening day of Little League. It was a big deal in town, with marching bands, and the teams, and people lined the streets as if it were Memorial Day.

Pittsford and environs hosted an antique car club. Men, mostly, with big old roadsters from the 1920s and '30s waxed to a deep black, or white, sheen. More than a dozen of them brought up the rear of the parade. A policeman was at the corner controlling traffic. As Tim and I drove up in my 1948, dusty but black Plymouth, Tim quickly put the top down. The cop looked at us, looked again. We waved and he ushered us behind the last antique vehicle, Karen Kurtz's father at the wheel, I was pretty sure.

As we headed up North Main Street, Tim, a University of Rochester graduate back from graduate work at the University of Oregon, took his shirt off and sat on the back of the car, his legs dangling over the back seat. He waved to the townspeople and they waved back. We came to 25 North Main and there was cousin Fran Zornow with her mother, my mother, Nanie and Una, Auntie, and others. I heard someone say "Why, look, there's Timmy! And Jimmy's driving! Wave, wave everybody!"

Tim and I waved back as we cruised slowly by. Then we were coming to the reviewing stand. The town supervisor, the mayor and other dignitaries were smiling and waving at their friends with their expensive roadsters, and then they saw us. We waved proudly as the men looked down with puzzled grimaces. When the parade turned left to head to the Little League field, Tim and I broke away and I drove him home. What a moment of unexpected fun.

One day in late August just before school started, a bunch of us were hanging out waiting for soccer practice to start. One of the guys I didn't let drive my car said to me so everyone could hear, "What do you and Sue do all the time?"

I just smiled back at him for a minute and then said, "We talk a lot."

"What about?"

"Everything."

And that was true. We talked mostly about small stuff, our own little world, but occasionally we'd dip into the issues of the universe. She took me to see my first musical, the movie "South Pacific." Like most of the suburban and rural expanse of western New York state, Pittsford was a sea of white people. There was a lot of frivolity in that movie starring Mitzi Gaynor and Rossano Brazzi. I was struck by the romance between the young lieutenant and the Polynesian girl; and the song by Rodgers and Hammerstein: "You've got to be Carefully Taught — to hate all the people your relatives hate."

You've got to be taught to be afraid

Of people whose eyes are oddly made,

And people whose skin is a diff'rent shade,

You've got to be carefully taught.

It seemed to me that if they loved each other, what did their nationality or color of their skin matter? It was that Aug. 28th when the nation was given a gift that would have an impact far beyond a song in a movie.

Martin Luther King Jr. was in Washington, D.C., at the Lincoln Memorial and electrified the nation with his "I Have a Dream" speech. I watched him on the nightly news and was stunned by the power, the moral authority, of his voice as he intoned: "I have a dream that one day this nation will rise up and live out the true meaning of its creed: 'We hold these truths to be self-evident: that all men are created equal'." Civil rights — the movement was years old — was barely discussed in our history and social studies classes. Slavery was written up in our textbooks as a "peculiar institution." The next day I ran into an older woman I loved and admired. I was excited and said to her, "Did you see Martin Luther King give his speech about his dream?"

This gracious, kind, loving lady screwed up her face and spat out, "Jimmy! Don't you listen to that nigger!"

At first I was speechless, then blurted out, "Don't you ever talk like that to me again!" I turned and marched off. I was 16 and I sought out my mother and told her about my run-in. She sighed heavily, sat down and said, "Oh Jimmy, Jimmy, I'm sorry you had to hear that. My generation, well, we just didn't know any better."

Just the year before, we had read Harper Lee's "To Kill a Mockingbird" in English class. The intelligence, innocence and energy of Jem; the utter competence as a father and a lawyer of Atticus; the cruel fate of Tom Robinson at the hands of ignorance and hate grabbed me by the shirt collar and shook me. The novel took me out of my protected little village and the discovery of racism troubled me deeply.

So how did Ann Hutchinson Smith know better? She did, and she raised her sons that way. Sue was at a disadvantage. Her parents were intelligent, good people, but like so many, if not most adults in suburban Rochester, they were not at all enamored with the civil rights movement. They did not believe in equality of the races.

Back in our own little teenage world, Sue and I began to squabble some that year, she a junior, me a senior. Sue was smart and popular, a sensual, pretty blonde. And she was wound tight. She carried an intensity that helped make her academically successful, but sometimes socially vulnerable. She too often and inexplicably lacked confidence for no good reason, because she had everything going for her. After more than a year of "going steady," we decided to give it a rest. I was relieved. She wanted to go out with Dick Bettinger in her class, the seventh man on the varsity basketball team behind Pete Menihan and me. Though I secretly never truly gave up on Carol Nobles, I knew she'd say no to going out on a date. I had my eye on the very popular, pretty and voluptuous Patsy Joyce, who said she'd love to go out with me.

"But what about Sue?" she asked.

"We broke up," I said. Patsy didn't quite believe it and she was right. By the end of the week, Sue and I decided we'd go ahead with our dates but then she said she wanted to get back together later that same night. I agreed and we promised to meet in her driveway at midnight. It meant telling our dates we had to be home by midnight. We were double-dating with my basketball teammate Bill Balden and his date. I stashed my Plymmy so I could make it to Elmwood Avenue on time. I had a grand time with Patsy, but I was itching to get to my car and drive to Sue's house. Bill dropped us off and Patsy slid in beside me as I headed to her house. Her parents weren't home and oh how I ached to go in there with her, but it was near midnight so I headed for 3485 Elmwood Avenue. Sue was waiting in her driveway. We hustled over under the big tree in her front yard and spent some time saying good night. Patsy wrote me a long note in my yearbook, ending with: "If you and Sue break up again for a day or two, let me know! Love, Patsy."

Sue's parents, Clark and Alice Hastings, were Rochester socialites and, at first, weren't too excited about their youngest daughter dating some poor kid from the farming village of Pittsford. I genuinely liked them, and eventually they came to like me. One summer weekend they invited my whole family for a cruise on Lake Ontario in their 42-foot yacht, the Flying Dutchman, which slept eight comfortably. Dad, who at least knew his one pair of shoes were not appropriate onboard, had to borrow my basketball sneakers. Once we were out on the waves my girlfriend whispered to me to go to the bow and open the hatch. There indeed was a treat, below she was smiling up at me while taking off her clothes and changing into her blue bathing suit.

It was, all in all, a successful adventure. I was invited to go on fishing trips with the Hastings where they hired guides and caught fish during long weekends at Cape Vincent or Henderson Harbor, near where the St. Lawrence River entered Lake Ontario. I think Clark enjoyed my company, but really what it meant to him is that, if I was there, then his daughter would be there too. They even hired me to be their gardener. And often Alice would have to yell out a window, "Susan, you leave Jim alone, he needs to weed that garden!"

It wasn't the only job I had in high school and it wasn't the only job where Sue would show up.

Two good men. Steve Williams and his son Stevie.

Chapter 17

Teens at Work

To say we idolized Teddy Zornow next door was putting it mildly. Eight years older — when I was 10, he was a high school basketball star, when I was 14, he was an All-American soccer player for the University of Rochester.

When we visited at Fisher's Cabin on Canandaigua Lake, where my grandparents honeymooned in 1906, fishing with Teddy was not a silent respite. No matter what he hooked, he'd whoop and holler, "Oh, it's a big one! Oh, it's a big one!"

If we spent the night, at breakfast the next morning he'd look at us and proclaim, "That's not a bowl, let me show you a cereal bowl," and he'd haul out a big salad bowl, fill it with cereal and munch it all down.

Teddy was larger than life. So when he called one Saturday afternoon — "Jim. I need your help, Steve too. There's rain coming and hay bales are still out in the field! — I couldn't wait to help him out. But Steve wasn't around. Ted told me to hurry up and think. "We'll need someone to drive the tractor."

I found Steve's friend Dave Hubregsen, who lived down the road from the hayfield. If I was 15, Dave was 12. Teddy got him up on the tractor seat, told him not to touch any gears, not to speed up or slow down, just "hold the steering wheel steady and when I tell you to, turn it slowly to the right."

Hubie was in awe and in seventh heaven. He grinned the whole time we circled that big field. Ted was on the wagon, I was running along, picking up bales and tossing them up to him. I picked up one bale and saw a mother mouse with a litter of tiny babies. I just couldn't expose them to the elements and so gently put that bale back down over them. This field was far from the barn and the mice would never get there, I theorized, running for the next bale to keep up with my cousin waiting on the wagon.

When we filled it, Ted would jump in the driver's seat, Hubie joined me atop the bales as we hurried back to the barn. The hay elevator wasn't in place and Teddy didn't want to take the time to set it up, so he and I threw the bales up into the loft, scurried up and stacked them, then rushed back out to the field for another load. We beat the rain. It was a great feeling of accomplishment for all three of us.

Teddy's father owned the farm with its cow herd, standard bred racing horses and more than 200 acres right in the middle of Pittsford. I'd end up working there for hourly pay summers and weekends, but my first full-time job was at Monroe Golf Club. Steve Williams, who married my cousin Ann Dowling, a gentle and generous woman, was the greens keeper. Steve was a demanding boss. He wanted his greens mowed perfectly. If you were raking sand traps, he wanted the sand smoothed with care. If you were watering greens or tees, it had to be exactly the right amount of water, not too much, not too little. He showed you, once, how to do all these things, and then he expected you to do them and do them right.

He also brought nepotism to new levels. He hired all of Ann's brothers, my cousins Tim, Dan and Tommy. He hired me and my brother Steve and then Bill and then Andy. And it was a good thing, because we could all use the paychecks. When you mastered one task, he'd trust you with more difficult work. Not everyone got to ride the tee mower, nor drive the small, energetic orange Worthington tractors. It's good Steve never caught Dan Dowling and me drag racing on either side of the 11th fairway on those tractors.

I always felt proud when I knew Steve was letting me handle more responsibility. I started working at the club when I turned 14, the age at which New York State allowed kids to work "farm jobs." Steve assured us that golf club work was classified under farm work. So, I started paying into Social Security. At 16, my third summer working for him, he let me work nights watering the greens, tees and fairways. It was a goal of mine because it paid a little more and also allowed for some daytime work too. In fact, without telling Steve, we set up a contest on who could make the most money in one week; in other words, who could work the most hours. He'd always sign our time cards, and overtime was almost an expectation.

Watering started at dusk, when the golfers were done. Down the middle of each fairway were valves set evenly with the manicured ground about 50 yards apart where you'd insert large sprinklers every hour on the hour. In the dark you'd find each valve with the help of the Cushman's headlight and get nine sprinklers going at once. It took about 40 minutes to set them all, leaving 20 minutes in between. In the middle of the night it could get a little scary, and so I started bringing my dog Yogi, a small brown and white bundle of energy. He loved it. He loved riding in the back of the three-wheeled motorized Cushman, and though I did, he didn't mind getting hit with the long spray from those sprinklers. On scheduled nights you'd also set sprinklers on the greens and tees.

Sue began to join us. She'd tell her parents she was sleeping over with a friend and we'd water together all night. We'd watch the moon move across the night sky, see the morning star appear big and bright, and watch the sky turn ever so light gray, announcing the coming of the dawn. And we did some other things in those 20 minutes before the next round of sprinkler changes.

But when the week of the contest came, I banned my girl and my dog because with the last round of watering I'd bring all the sprinklers back into the barn at 6 a.m. The morning greens-cutting crew came in at 7. In contest week, I put away the sprinklers and grabbed a greens mower.

Guys would stay past 3 p.m. and do an extra round of late-afternoon raking of sand traps, or go out and "rotarize," the hated task of mowing the rough with rotary mowers, kicking up dust between the clusters of pine trees. But we were racking up hours. I was aiming to win the contest. I wanted to put three 48-hour weeks into one week. That would be 144 hours. I figured that since there are 168 hours in a week, and though I'd work essentially three shifts a day, there would still be time for three hours of sleep each day. I could do that for one week.

And I did. And I won. Our regular work week was eight hours a day Monday-Friday, five hours Saturday morning and three hours Sunday morning. That week I worked triple and got paid triple. Instead of the usual $79, my paycheck was $237 that week. Steve never questioned it, but we didn't do it again.

He had a permanent crew of two or three men working year-round, but I think he genuinely enjoyed supervising teenagers, and 20-something college students. I'll always be grateful to him.

But my sixth summer at the club went bad. If something happened on the overnight watering job, like a valve was clogged and you couldn't fix it, you were supposed to leave Steve a note. One night, besides the fairways, I was also watering greens and tees, but I couldn't get the 13th tee valve to work. I forgot to leave him a note, in fact I forgot to tell him, since I stayed on that morning to rake sand traps.

I was in the middle of a trap and he roared up in his pickup truck. "What happened at 13!" he yelled. He was mad. Remembering, I felt awful and said, "I'm sorry Steve. I couldn't get it to work. I forgot to tell you."

The very short grass of greens and tees is sensitive to hot days, and it was hot. Steve had to pretty much flood the 13th tee to keep it from burning, which he said in no uncertain terms and then told me he can't trust me and he'd have to let me go. Then he roared off.

I was stunned. I'd been doing good work for him for several summers. I was standing in the sand trap with the rake and decided to finish it. Then he drove back, got out of the cab and said I could keep working days, but I couldn't water nights anymore.

I should have said fine. He was right. I was wrong. But it didn't feel right to stay where I wasn't trusted, so I said, "Well, no. I'll finish this trap and leave."

He drove off. I finished, walked back to the barn, filled out my time card and left him some sort of note defending myself. I walked along Golf Avenue, got to the Zornows' farm, and walked down the lane looking for Roger Powers. He had married Teddy's sister Betsy and they took over the farm. Teddy moved with his father to a big new horse farm they bought to start their own line of racehorses. I found Roger and asked if he needed any help for the rest of the summer. He said sure.

The next day I went to the farm instead of the golf club. My firing caused quite a stir in the family and I was sorry about that because Steve had always been so generous and so good to me, my brothers and my cousins. I should have remembered to tell him that tee needed watering. But now, I was a farmhand.

Working the farm. Charlie Corby, Roger Powers, Jim and Steve Smith, Ted Zornow at Roger's wedding to cousin Betsy Zornow.

Chapter 18

The Farm

In high school Roger Powers, like his girlfriend Betsy Zornow, were four years ahead of me. She was a pretty and full-of-pep cheerleader, he a star soccer player and the fastest guy in the school. He ran the 100-yard dash in almost 10 seconds flat. Part Blackfoot Sioux, he was tawny, rugged and handsome. They went to separate colleges, Betsy to Geneseo State to be a teacher. Her first job was at Allen Creek School. Roger went to Alfred State and studied agriculture and also served a stint in the Navy as a submariner. It intrigued me that a young man who spent so much time at sea came back to work the land. I don't think he ever lost his sea legs. I asked him once how fast his nuclear submarine could go under water. He deadpanned, "That's classified."

When Roger and Betsy got married, I was in their wedding party. They made a beautiful couple. Betsy's father, Theodore J. Zornow, was developing a new line of standard breds on a new farm in Caledonia, some 30 miles away, and his son Teddy was with him. The father was a board member of the United States Trotting Association for 27 years and its president from 1970 to 1977.

Roger took over managing the farm in Pittsford. There was a dairy store right on the farm where the milk from its large herd was pasteurized and sold. Ted's daughter Carol, and her husband Charlie Corby, who had been an All-County basketball player at Pittsford High, managed the dairy.

At least four kids I grew up with lived on farms: Kathy Hopkins, Hal Lusk, David Knickerbocker and Ray Wallman. Ray was tough, an All-American wrestler in high school. He and Hal and I played on the Lions together in Little League. Hal was a year older and taught me how to be a catcher. His family dates back to the late 1780s in Pittsford. When he grew up, Hal sold the farm. Home prices are upwards of $600,000 out where his hay fields used to be.

The Hopkins family also goes back to the beginnings of white settlement. Caleb Hopkins came from Pittsford, Vt., in 1791. He was the first town supervisor of Pittsford, N.Y. The Hopkins Farm today is listed in the National Register of Historic Places at the corner of Clover Street and Calkins Road. They sold the development rights to the town so the family can keep farming. So did the Knickerbockers. Suburban sprawl surrounds their farm on Knickerbocker Hill, and when newer families complain to David about the noise and the smell, "I just tell them we were here first," he says with a big grin.

Pittsford Farms, where I was employed summers, had been a huge playground for us kids. We ranged all over those 200-plus acres. In the winter we sledded down the hill in the cow pasture. Summers featured a cart pulled by a pony named Black Beauty. We would all pile in for rides around the farm. When we were a little older, Carol let her youngest sister Fran and me ride her horse, a frisky chestnut brown gelding. We'd trot him to the end of the lane and when we turned back toward the barn, that horse always broke into a gallop for the rides of our lives.

The lane belongs in a bucolic rural America landscape painting. Little more than a dirt trail wide enough for a tractor and wagon, there are pastures on each side. It is lined by big old maple trees, their limbs creating a stunning canopy of colors in the fall. In the summer of circa 1965 they needed tending. The limbs were getting so low that the hay wagons barely fit through.

My first day on the job, the day after I left the golf club, Roger handed me a chain saw about as big as I was. He told me to climb up in the trees and cut off the lower limbs. He also supplied me with a rope, then went off in his pickup truck. Roger is the kind of man who would never ask a worker to do anything he wouldn't do. But Roger's biceps were bigger than mine.

I checked the oil and gas, tied the rope on the handle, climbed up into the first tree and pulled up the chain saw. I had never yanked the starter rope on a chain saw while sitting on a tree limb and I was a little nervous.

"I can do this," I told myself. First I climbed higher than the lowest branches, then I decided to stand up on a branch rather than sit. I set the choke, pulled a few times and the thing roared to life. I carefully put the blade on the nearest low limb and neatly cut it off; then the next and the next. When one tree was done, I'd climb down and go to the next tree — all afternoon, up the lane until the job was done. I stood there, my arms and legs aching, and looked back at the barn. There was more than enough room for hay wagons to get through and still those maples were majestic. Roger came along and helped me throw the downed branches into his truck.

On one side of the lane was the cow pasture. The biggest single job I had was putting a new fence around it. Roger showed up with locust posts, maybe 150 of them. He and I put the new ones on the ground next to the old ones still standing in the ground. He left me with a shovel, and a red Farmall tractor with a large drill attached to the back. Thank God for the drill. I dug around the old posts, loosened them and pulled them out. Then I'd back the tractor up, place the drill above the old hole, drill down three to four feet, put the new post in, get the shovel and fill in around it. Post after post, around some three acres of pasture. Then Roger and I stretched the wire fencing and nailed it into each post, top to bottom. Locust lasts. A half-century later those posts are still good.

But Roger wasn't going to concentrate on dairy farming. He and Betsy were going to take the business in a different direction. He planted sweet corn, acres and acres of it. Actually, he showed me how to plant corn and I did it; pour the kernels in tubs on a contraption with two wheels you pulled behind a tractor. This particular Farmall corn planter had six canisters, so we planted six rows of corn at a time. It plugged the kernels just the right depth into the soil and the right space between each, six rows at a time.

When the stalks grew above your head with the ripened ears of corn, we'd start out at 6 a.m. carrying burlap sacks, picking one ear at a time. By the time you got halfway down the first row, you were soaked with the dew from the corn stalks. I calculated that I picked 10,000 ears of corn the three summers I worked on the farm.

I planted melons, too. First you'd lay down black plastic strips and push soil over them so the plastic wouldn't blow away. Then about every two feet, you'd cut into the plastic with a trowel, dig a small hole and insert a small melon plant. Harvesting the ripe, hefty musk melons was also one at a time, bending over and picking them off their vines.

That first year Betsy and Roger sold their crops from a truck at the corner of Golf Avenue and Marsh Road. They eventually built an impressive market — Powers Farm Market, still a mainstay of the Pittsford economy where people from miles around go to shop.

The hardest farm work was always baling hay to feed the cows. It seemed that whenever we were baling hay it was the muggiest, hottest day with the sun mercilessly beating down on you. God bless Sue Hastings, who showed up on many of those days with jugs of chilled lemonade.

Milking the cows was inside work, but still with its challenges. The milking machines were large stainless steel containers with four suction cups you'd attach to each of the cows' nipples. There was always soothing music coming from a radio, as research showed that cows produced more and richer milk while listening to easy music.

Farmhands poured the milk from the stainless steel containers into milk cans that stood about thigh high and held 10 gallons. Full, they were heavy. We had a cart with two car tires on it that held four cans of milk.

The dairy was up a slight incline along a paved walk maybe 50 yards from the cow barn door. I'd need a running start in the barn, make a hard right turn out the door and run up the walk pushing that cart. Without the running start, I'd never make it to the dairy and was always slowing to a crawl before reaching the dairy door.

Inside was a big stainless steel pasteurizing cauldron. Charlie and Carol Corby were running the dairy. Charlie and I would pick up a milk can and pour it in. We were milking some 60 cows, twice a day. Plastic tubing channeled the milk from the pasteurizer to the bottling operation. The glass quart bottles stamped with "Pittsford Farms Dairy" moved along a belt where they were automatically filled and then capped. We'd pick the bottles off the end of the belt, put them in metal crates and carry them into the stand-up cooler. One day Charlie told me to grab a gallon of concentrated chocolate to make several crates of bottled chocolate milk. But I grabbed a gallon of eggnog concentrate instead, which I didn't notice until I opened it. Charlie didn't want to try to sell eggnog in July, so he made me take it home, taking its cost, $7, out of my weekly pay. The Smiths drank homemade eggnog all summer.

I liked putting the newly pasteurized and bottled milk in the cooler and carefully placing a bottle at a time on the shelf for sale. If my timing was right, I'd be placing the bottles on the shelf when the glass door would open on the other side and there would be my grandmother, taking down bottles to sell.

"Why, hello, Jimmy," Nanie would say and smile. And I'd smile back and say, "Hi Nanie."

On Saturdays at noon I'd drive her up to 25 North Main Street. Sometimes my mother's sister and next-door neighbor Margaret Zornow would be there too, but usually it was my mother, my grandmother and me (I don't remember where my brothers were). She would have Ritz crackers and cheese. Sometimes she'd make cheese rarebit that we'd put over crackers or bread. Sometimes it would be tuna with lettuce or grilled cheese sandwiches. And there would usually be pie for dessert, a cream pie or custard or meringue pie.

And always, always there would be tea — in a little brown teapot. She'd have sugar and she'd pour cream into a little light blue vase. We would have gentle conversation. Then I'd drive Nanie back to the dairy, which closed at 5 p.m. on Saturdays. Like Powers Farm Market out on Marsh Road, Pittsford Farms Dairy had loyal customers who drove to South Main Street to buy their milk.

Most of the horses had been moved to Ted's Avon Farms. But Concho Hanover, a renowned New York state trotter and sire to several champion standard breds, was still at Pittsford Farms. One summer he was entrusted to me. I fed him, I mucked out his stall, I made sure he got exercise in the fenced-in pasture and, at the end of each day, I put him in his stall. He was a huge, dark brown horse. His racing days over, Concho was out to stud. A couple of times that summer Teddy would bring a mare around. My job was to hold the mare, who was supposed to be in heat. Ted would help Concho with his duties. This was outside in the barnyard. Well, it seemed to me the mare wasn't always ready, but Concho was. Teddy held a rope attached to his halter, but there really wasn't any stopping him. The mare would throw her head and neigh and move to the side as Concho used his body, pushing her to where he wanted her. Then I realized, she was being coy and after a while she was ready and Concho mounted her from behind. It was all over in a matter of minutes.

As the summer wore on, Concho and I became friends. He would get frisky with me, nibble at me as I brushed him down each day. But we got to trusting each other. Trotters pull sulkies and are never ridden. No one ever rode Concho. The summer was ending and I was going back to college. On my last day, I brought my little brother Andy down to Concho's paddock. Andy was in kindergarten or first grade and I told him I wanted him to see this great horse. I led Concho over to the fence where Andy could put his hand through and feed him carrots. It was right where a tree limb hung over. My plan was to be the first person to ever ride Concho Hanover and I was being especially attentive to him that morning. He was enjoying Andy's carrots as I climbed to the top of the fence, grabbed the tree limb and, hand-over-hand, positioned myself right over the horse. When I let go, I'd fall about 18 inches down onto Concho's back.

"Watch this, Andy," I said and dropped down. Concho instantly reared up on his hind legs, then bucked forward onto his front legs, throwing me right over his shoulders. I literally summersaulted into the air and landed on the ground on my back.

"Are you OK, Jimmy?" said my startled little brother.

I looked up and Concho was looking straight down at me, as if to say, "What were you thinking?"

I got up, brushed myself off, patted the horse and said, "Sorry, buddy, but I had to try." Then I walked Andy home. Good thing Roger never found out.

Graduation from PCS in 1964 with cousin Janie Dowling.

Chapter 19

Mischief

Hanging out at Hicks & McCarthy's was a Pittsford pastime since the soda fountain opened on South Main Street in 1913. Babe and his brother Norm and wife Eloise Hicks and their son Tommy, who pitched for the Lions in Little League when I was the catcher, and Larry McCarthy and his daughter Peggy came from the same Irish clan I did — the Finucanes of Ballylongford, County Kerry, Ireland. Hicks & McCarthy's was the place to be, inside at the counter with a 10-cent cherry Coke pressed out of separate syrup dispensers topped off with seltzer water, and a burger for 25 cents; or outside watching the girls go by.

Mostly it was just being sociable. Sometimes, though, hanging out at Hicks bred mischief, like the time my classmate Jim Tolman persuaded his older brother to let him take the family car, parked nearby. Bad idea. Jim didn't yet have his license, but a bunch of us climbed in for a joy ride, including my cute cousin Mary Ann Hutchinson, my Uncle Brud's daughter. The radio was cranked, we were whirring through back roads and wound our way to Mitchell Road with its one-lane bridge over the canal, the road of my first memory — my mother pushing me in the teeter-tot.

A strange feeling descended over me. It was like slow motion and me wrestling with myself about whether or not to tell Tolman to slow down. He sped onto the bridge and then — crash! — the right side of the car sliced into the bridge railings, the noise was deafening. We emerged on the other side of the bridge and went down the embankment and came to a stop. Everyone jumped out, miraculously no one was injured. Adrenalin took over and I ran. I ran toward the little house where my parents first brought me after I was born in the hospital. Then I stopped, said, "What am I doing?" and ambled back to the scene of the crash.

Mary Ann said something like everyone is OK.

Jim kept saying, "What am I going to tell my brother?" In those days before cellphones, someone came along and offered assistance. Eventually a tow truck came. Jim later told us that he convinced his older brother Tom to say that he was driving. That is one good older brother.

About this same time, early spring of my junior year, 1963, I asked my father to let me take his Ford Falcon station wagon with a friend who would drive because he had his license. Well, I drove and picked up five or six guys and a case of beer. We were cruising down French Road when I saw a sheriff's car in the rear-view mirror. I drove slowly, too slowly.

His red lights flicked on. I pulled over. Everyone was tossing beer bottles out the right-side doors. When the cop came to the driver's window, I saw that it was Jarvis. He was always one of the cops who broke up our break-in basketball games at Lincoln Avenue School.

He asked me to step out of the car. Then he told me to get in his car. I was sure we were heading to jail.

"You're Jim Smith's son, aren't you?" he said as he turned onto Monroe Avenue and headed toward the village. "25 North Main Street, right?" he asked.

I told him yes. He pulled into our driveway, walked me to my door, up the stairs, right into our living room where Mom and Dad and my little brothers were watching "Gun Smoke." I watched Steve and Bill on the floor look up bug-eyed at Jarvis' revolver, the handle sticking out of his holster.

He and my father spoke, Jarvis left, and then Dad was leading me down the hallway to our bedroom.

I heard Mom say, "Jim, don't you hurt him!"

He was angry. He had his fist in my face. Then he hauled off and slammed it into my upper arm — a harmless jab, really. He would never really hit me, but he wanted to let me know how mad he was. I think Jarvis drove him to get his car. The guys had all walked away carrying as much of the beer as they could.

When I wasn't on a team, I drifted. I disappointed my parents and, really, I disappointed myself.

Senior year, with my own cool car, making all the varsity teams, elected co-captain of the baseball team, a steady girl, I quit the mischief. I certainly never was inducted into the National Honor Society like my cousin Katie Kinsky, but I was voted into the Boy's Leaders Club and I joined the cast in our senior play. Ray Wallman and Lefty Dalton talked me into trying out with them for a part as a lark. They got what they wanted, cameo appearances as walk-ons. Trouble is, I got a speaking part, playing a hard-drinking reporter in "The Man Who Came to Dinner." I found myself spending hours and hours memorizing my lines. My cousin Janie Dowling was in the make-up crew. She caked my face, fixed my fedora to the right angle and cheerfully gave me encouragement before I went on stage.

At graduation that June, it was Janie and I who received the two biggest awards, $400 and $500 scholarships from local organizations for leadership, scholarship, community involvement and, as the letter to me stated, "It was also felt that you would have some need." We were called up to the stage separately, to the applause of our fellow graduates. That money was enough to cover my tuition freshman year. Nanie, our grandmother, proudly had her picture taken with us after the ceremonies. Janie was headed to Ithaca College on nearly a full scholarship. I was going to Brockport State on student loans; many of them, as you know, I passed along to my father, starting with the five hundred bucks at graduation.

Dan Dowling in country

Chapter 20

Vietnam

A handful of boys I grew up with went off to war in Vietnam, including three cousins — David Hutchinson, whose father, Jack, would later display his son's many combat medals at family gatherings; Dan Dowling, who could barely bring himself to shoot at another human being; my blood-brother Andy Conine, who always made jokes when we'd play army as kids, and who came back from the war a very damaged man — and my friend Mel Morgan, whom I once raised turtle doves with, who didn't come back.

In 1964 my guess is that most Americans had no idea where Vietnam was. About 200 American "advisers" had been killed there. At Brockport State my freshman year I answered a student poll question on what the U.S. should do about the mounting danger there with: "bomb the Communists" into submission. It was just that August that Congress passed the infamous Tonkin Gulf resolution stating that North Vietnamese naval vessels had "deliberately and repeatedly attacked United States naval vessels" and giving President Johnson authority "to take all necessary steps, including the use of armed force" to defend our allies in Southeast Asia, i.e. South Vietnam.

Senator Wayne Morse, Democrat of Oregon, was one of only two senators to oppose what he called "this aggressive course of action."

"We are kidding the world," he said. North Vietnamese gunboats fired torpedoes and automatic weapons at the USS Maddox in the Gulf of Tonkin in international waters off the coast of North Vietnam once, but there were grave doubts about whether they attacked a second time.

A year later we had 81,400 soldiers in the country and 509 killed in action.

David Hutchinson came back alive and decorated. My mother adored her older brother Jack. He raised his family in the village a few blocks from our home. As young boys, his son David and I played all the time. Sometimes we'd let his sisters Margot and Linda join us, but they were perfectly happy ignoring us too. By high school, however, David had no interest in sports and that's about all I was interested in. Pittsford in the early 1960s was not a big high school but David and I barely saw each other. I went to college. He went to Southeast Asia. He moved to Florida when he got back and has a successful career selling large recreational boats.

Janie Dowling and I grew up together. She went off to Ithaca College and I went to Brockport State. Her brothers went off to different worlds. She reminded me of that in a descriptive letter from Ithaca May 13, 1967; by then, more than 400,000 American soldiers were in Vietnam.

"I was looking at the big globe in our library the other day — looking at Vietnam and at Panama," she wrote. "I put one finger on Panama and tried to reach the other hand to Vietnam but they wouldn't even quite reach. Panama and Vietnam are just about half a world away from each other."

Tim Dowling was a Peace Corps volunteer in Panama. Dan was drafted into the Army. One brother in peace work; the other at war. By then I was against the war, part of a growing cascade of "young people," "draft dodgers," "hippies" in a societal gulf known as the "generation gap." Our fathers had fought in WW II and most in their generation could not abide their children challenging the wisdom of our leaders.

Dan doesn't talk much about Vietnam. He has said, "I couldn't kill another human being." He did shoot at the moon one night. Dan always has marched to his own drum.

He told me of a night in an outpost half a mile from his base. "It was about midnight when I told my friend Cranert the moon was so close that I could hit it. I fired my M-16 at the moon.

"We immediately heard the guys stationed at the outpost half a mile in the opposite direction from the base screaming that they were under attack. They were told to hightail it back to base. We asked if we could return to base also. They told us that the incoming fire was not near us, and we should stay at our post," Dan told me. "I decided not to tell them the incoming fire was me firing at the moon."

It was the most he had ever said to me about the war. When I pressed him a little, he cautiously talked of "being the point man" in treks through the jungle. When attacks came, "you couldn't see them, you couldn't tell where they were shooting from. I did not desire to kill another person, even the enemy. But, need be, I would not have hesitated. Fortunately, I was never in such a situation. In the various firefights we were involved in, we never actually saw the Viet Cong."

He sent me a picture of him with some boys, along with a note: "Hoa, a natural born leader, and Tan, one of the brightest kids I ever knew," wrote Dan, 40 years after his tour of duty. "This picture is the real story of my Vietnam experience. These kids and seven or eight of their friends ate breakfast with us, worked and played with us, and I frequently spent evenings at their homes drinking bah-mui-bah beer.

"It was very unusual for soldiers to be friends with the kids. In fact, most soldiers disliked and mistrusted all the Vietnamese people. But, when given the chance, these kids were personable, trustworthy, funny, and very happy, even though they lived in the middle of a war.

"We took over half the village of Rach Kien, about 30 miles south of Saigon in the Mekong Delta. A small river split the village and we lived in the hooch closest to the kids' homes. Whenever the choppers brought us back from a mission, the kids would be sitting on the roof of our hooch and they would cheer for us. My relationship with these kids and their families is what made my experience special and separated me from the rest of the troops," Dan wrote.

It didn't surprise me. Cousin Dan was always good with kids, playing games with them at family picnics, telling jokes, just like his father, Tom, who seemed always to have a gaggle of children around him.

When Dan returned from the war, he enrolled at Brockport State and spent a career teaching math in Rochester high schools. He and my brother Steve built a beautiful cabin on the Cedar River in the Adirondack Mountains. Dan is like a brother, and when we go to Canandaigua each summer, he usually joins us.

As a young man, Andy Conine also joined us at Canandaigua. Born just two months apart, we grew up together. The son of a farmer, he helped show me how to bale hay. From the beginning, Andy was always filled with humor, double entendres, jokes that made us all laugh to the point of rolling on the floor. But when we were playing guns, serious army exploits, we'd be stern with him, usually to little effect — he'd roll his eyes, pretend his air rifle was broken and generally break ranks. Andy was the unlikeliest of soldiers.

Super smart, he somehow managed to bust out of the Rochester Institute of Technology. The draft board got him and he went to Vietnam. Friends and family have whispered about different things that happened. And he dribbled stuff out. Mostly he wouldn't talk about it.

One night he told me that he was on top of outdoor showers, pouring water into holding tanks. Some of his buddies were showering — "then incoming hit. The mortar rounds exploded so close I was thrown off, maybe 25 feet. When I came to, the showers were gone. So were those guys."

After that, he had written home to one friend that, "I I I I I can't can't can't can't can't think think think think think anymore anymore anymore anymore anymore."

But when he got back he was able to enroll in Cornell University's agriculture program, graduate and spend many years advising farmers in western New York on best practices. He got married to a wonderful young woman while he was still at Cornell. I visited their apartment and sat at their dining room table.

"Nice chairs, Jim, don't ya think?" he said.

I agreed.

"Well, we needed new chairs. So one day at Cornell I put on my dungarees, hung keys from my belt, pulled my pickup truck up to the library, went in and got these chairs. I took them one at a time, all six of them, and set them in the truck. A librarian actually held the door for me once. Told her we were going to refinish them." He grinned at me.

Andy not only got an Ivy League degree, but also his new dining room chairs from Cornell.

We were young men. Andy barely made it to middle age. He drank and drank more and couldn't stop. He functioned. He worked, but the drinking got worse. No one could reach him; not his parents, not his brother nor his sisters, not me — his blood brother — not his wife.

We smoked marijuana occasionally, he and I. One bright afternoon at his father's farm we were stoned when he stopped me in the driveway and asked me to look up at a tall maple tree. "See the green leaves. Way up, the very top of the tree. All the way up. Find the leaf that is the highest of them all. See how it is etched against the blue sky. Look closely. See it. Follow its green outline against the blue sky. See it? Always do that," he told me.

I do.

The last time I saw him he was swigging gin straight from a bottle he pulled out from under the front seat of his car. I took a swig too. I knew I couldn't argue with him anymore.

Hundreds of people, hundreds, showed up at his funeral. He was 39.

He never met Mel Morgan. Mel lived literally across the tracks. His house was across the street from the pickle factory, where it always stunk. One summer he and I got some cages and a few turtle doves and put them in Una's barn. She said that was fine. We fed them cracked corn. Mel would talk to them gently and they would coo back. At the end of the summer he proposed releasing them, so we made a ceremony out of it, he and I. We brought the cages out into my backyard, gently held the birds in our hands and just let them go, two at a time. They flew away. Mel smiled.

In his front yard was a tall maple tree filled with green-winged seeds among the leaves. You could break them neatly in half. As they dropped, they whirled like helicopters down to the ground. Mel and I would sit up in the high limbs and over and over watch them whirl as they fell to the ground.

In sixth grade we were watching a film in the auditorium about the Battle of Gettysburg. Mel could be a wiseguy. After a particularly gruesome scene of dead Civil War soldiers, he yelled out, "Good fertilizer!"

Sixth-grade teacher Sid Ludwig, a tall, broad-shouldered but kindly man, walked over to where Mel was sitting and knocked him in the head with his big college ring, its cut green jewel drawing blood.

Mel was the third baseman for the American Legion team in Little League and, like Jimmie Palmer, he was a fearless hitter. But he didn't play sports in high school. He worked. After graduation when I went off to Brockport State, he came up to see me one night. He came to say good-bye before he went to Vietnam. We went out and had some beers, then he drove back to Pittsford.

In Vietnam he became a helicopter gunner. He re-upped for a second tour. He'd stand at the open door firing a big machine gun, until his helicopter was shot down and he was killed.

After a decade of war, 58,190 other Americans had been killed, along with an estimated three million Vietnamese.

We finally stopped fighting there in 1973. One of the war's architects, Defense Secretary Robert S. McNamara, published his memoir in 1995, "In Retrospect, The Tragedy and Lessons of Vietnam" wherein he wrote: "I concede with painful candor and a heavy heart . . . hindsight proves us wrong" about Vietnam. His contemporary, Secretary of State Dean Rusk, for one, never acknowledged that the war was wrong. When Walter Cronkite finally opposed the war at the end of his nightly broadcast on Feb. 27, 1968: "To say that we are closer to victory today is to believe, in the face of the evidence, the optimists who have been wrong in the past. But it is increasingly clear to this reporter that the only rational way out then will be to negotiate, not as victors, but as an honorable people who lived up to their pledge to defend democracy, and did the best they could." Lyndon Johnson told an aide that he had lost Middle America. He decided not to run again — too many voters opposed his war — and we elected Richard Nixon with his secret plan to end the war.

McNamara's stunning mea culpa addressed the fate of those Americans "who served in Vietnam and never returned."

"Does the unwisdom of our intervention nullify their effort and their loss? I think not. They did not make the decisions. They answered their nation's call to service. They went in harm's way on its behalf. And they gave their lives for their country and its ideals. That our effort in Vietnam proved unwise does not make their sacrifice less noble."

Maybe so, but after my knee-jerk, naïve opinion as a freshman I joined the growing cacophony of mostly young citizens who rose up in opposition to the war. I saw no reason why Americans should be dying in Vietnam. I believed our leaders were not being truthful with us and I deplored Nixon's secret war in Cambodia. Since when does the U.S. secretly invade another country?

Though I paid my own way through college, I knew I was among the privileged in America safely deferred from the draft. When I graduated, my first job, as a history teacher — including the history of Southeast Asia — kept me exempt from the battlefields.

So many wise voices spoke to me — Martin Luther King, Jr., minister William Sloane Coffin, Yale Divinity School Associate Dean Michael Allen, the radical lawyer William Kunstler, radical priests Philip and Daniel Berrigan (I didn't think they were radical, but that is how they were described in the press). They believed there were many, many problems at home — poverty, ignorance, racial hatred — that needed our energies to solve rather than wasting a generation of young men and women in an unjust war.

Poets and essayists, journalists and balladeers like Joan Baez and Bob Dylan gave rise to ever-growing protests in the streets against the war. Peter, Paul and Mary, one melodic voice in the protest movement, sang:

Where have all the soldiers gone, long time passing?
Where have all the soldiers gone, long time ago?
Where have all the soldiers gone?
Gone to graveyards, every one.
When will they ever learn?
When will they ever learn?

With Tom Lawson at a beer blast. Mimi Tcheou. With Sue Hastings at graduation 1968.

Chapter 21

Brockport State

Ann and Jim Smith drove their oldest son to college in late August, 1964. Ann had managed one year at Nazareth College before dropping out to marry her Army Air Corps bomber pilot in 1944. I arrived a little more than a year after World War II ended, part of the first wave of the Baby Boom generation. Though she had followed her young handsome man from an air base in the Deep South up to Madison, Wisc., it was family lore that, from her earliest years, Ann Hutchinson Smith got nervous whenever she left the confines of the Village of Pittsford. Brockport was only 35 miles away, but Ann Smith at age 40 felt like she was leaving her first son on the other side of the world. Throughout my time in college I would receive several letters a week from my mother, letters of great perception, wisdom, humor and advice.

This bright day under a blue sky for freshmen arrivals at the State University of New York, College at Brockport, I pulled a suitcase and a small trunk out of my parents' car. We found my room at the end of a narrow hallway on the second floor of Bramley Hall. We met my two roommates, I picked the top bunk and I walked Mom and Dad back to their car. He shook my hand, Mom gave me a longer than normal hug, and I watched them drive away, back to Pittsford and my three younger brothers.

I had never been away from home for longer than a weekend. Except for one high school soccer teammate a year ahead of me, I didn't know a soul among the 2,000 students (it would double to 4,000 by my senior year). I remembered my guidance counselor saying, "Jimmy, are you sure you want to go to college?" Well, there I was facing a full course load of required freshman courses and excited about the prospect of playing soccer for a storied college team.

I found I fit easily into the freshman team and met a lot of guys just like me, white kids from mostly little upstate school districts intent on succeeding in college athletics and getting a teaching degree. Not all of us would make it. There were four dorms in our building. Our first formal meeting was hosted by the director of housing, a barrel-chested man with a crew cut who boasted of helping to build the New York State Thruway back in the 1950s. He told us to look to our left and to our right because, "before the end of this year one of those guys sitting next to you will flunk out." He was right. One of my roommates flunked out after the first semester.

From 1964 to 1968 Brockport State wasn't exactly at the forefront of what we have come to know as "The Sixties." Halfway between Rochester and Buffalo at the edge of a small village with a Main Street much like Pittsford's — except there was a movie theater and several bars — Brockport, N.Y. wasn't anything like Berkeley or Columbia or the other campuses that manifested Bob Dylan's "The Times They Are a Changin'." There were plenty of Ph.D.s on the faculty, but most seemed like holdovers from a distant era.

My freshman English professor, Mr. Chestnut (no Ph.D.), a tall, thin, bald man with a tanned but wrinkled face, scolded me one day early in the semester for coming to class with my shirt untucked. I was truly shocked that he said such a thing. I thought, "What is this, grade school?" and told him that I wouldn't tuck in my shirt. Then I sat down in my seat. Freshmen were assigned to class alphabetically, and there were lots of students in my classes with names beginning with "R," "S" and "T"; They all sat there in silence as I took out my notebook and pen with — God forsake me — my shirt untucked.

For some reason Mr. Chestnut let it go. But when I got my next essay back he had given it an "F" and scrawled on it, "Mr. Smith, you think you can write but you can't!"

I had never really considered that I could write, but if he thought I thought I could, I decided to give it more consideration. He didn't give me a passing grade for the rest of the semester and assigned me to remedial writing class, a requirement if a professor sent you there.

Two good things came of it: I concentrated, really for the first time in my life, about putting one word after another on paper, and Mimi Tcheou showed up there too. I was struck by the beauty of this diminutive Asian-American girl with long black hair who was in all my classes. Sue Hastings, entering her senior year at Pittsford Central, and I had pledged fidelity, but then each day at Brockport brought into view more and more pretty college co-eds. I was captivated by Elizabeth "Mimi" Tcheou, who was from New York City. I had never met anyone from New York City.

I suspected she voluntarily enrolled in remedial writing, because we had begun to flirt and write notes to each other. She wrote like a dream. And I found out she could kiss like a dream too. Remedial writing was at night in majestic Hartwell Hall, the college's original building, with an impressive white bell tower topping the three stories of ivy-covered brick walls. When class was over we'd stroll under the large maples on campus and were soon embracing beneath bright stars shining through the branches. She had a perfectly proportioned body: shapely legs, a tiny waist, firm stand-up little breasts and full, inviting lips. My generation had moved beyond the twist on the dance floor, and oh how Mimi could move to the music of the Rolling Stones and the Beatles. I was a little awkward and clunky to the new beat, but then we discovered a different musical haven.

The only reason I went to music class at 8 a.m. was because I knew she would be there. The professor would assign classical music pieces to listen to. We'd go to the library, sign out a 33-rpm record and place it on a turntable in one of several soundproof booths. With the door shut I'd sit in a chair, she would climb in my lap and we would make out to Respighi, Beethoven and Liszt. Ah, but this was Brockport, 1964, and one day a stern librarian opened the door on us and said the listening booths were for serious study, certainly not what we were doing. So we found other places.

On a warm night early in that first semester we found ourselves strolling on the athletic fields. We sat down in the grass and she leaned over and kissed me. Then she smiled up at me and we let nature take over, until my Catholic guilt arrived.

She sighed and put her pretty face in the nape of my neck and held me for a long time. We unraveled and slowly got up. I took her hand and held it all the way back to her dorm room. I don't remember a word we said, but it was pretty clear to me we were both lost in each other. I even took her to Pittsford to meet my parents.

I ended the semester with all C's and an F in English. The Dean of Men, Mr. Welch, called and told me to come to his office. He was a slight man, 30-ish with thick glasses that made him look a little like an owl. He was gentle, almost fatherly, and asked why I was getting only C's, and with the F, a 1.8 GPA. I told him Mr. Chestnut didn't like me and I asked him, seriously, what's wrong with C's.

He was calm and let my question sit there for a moment. First, he said, Mr. Chestnut was an experienced, respected teacher and he sent me to remedial class for a reason. Then he said staying below a 2.0 GPA could prevent me from playing soccer. But more importantly, it's a competitive world and C's aren't enough to succeed in this world, Mr. Welch said. He wanted to see me do better next semester.

What Dean Welch did was make me think about learning. I used to pass courses, most of them boring, I thought, so I could play sports. Except for history classes — I always soaked up history — I didn't learn for learning's sake. It wasn't just the dean who was giving me pause. I knew my parents weren't all that pleased. All my life, I wanted them to be proud of me. The very words "college education" became more real to me. That spring semester of freshman year I raised my grades to two A's, two B's and two C's, a 2.8 GPA.

Mimi was still in most of my classes and we loved that. At the same time I had this lingering guilt that I was cheating on Sue, but I was simply stricken by this waif of a Chinese girl who was spending more and more time with me.

My mother, with three younger sons at home, found the time to write me long, amusing, supportive letters in her graceful handwriting. Near the end of my second semester freshman year she was feeling protective of

Sue, or maybe more concerned about her son's behavior. She could write great little scenes from 25 North Main Street, like how my brothers at that moment "are fighting over the television. It won't work for a whole program anyhow. Now they are fighting over where they will sit. Sometimes I wonder how I stand you guys. You overwhelm me."

I was overwhelming her from afar just then and she gave me a good scolding in her letter May 11, 1965. Sue Hastings had called her.

Jim, I just don't understand how you can feel it is alright for you to act as though Sue is your girl, your very steady girl, how can you believe it yourself — and make her — expect her, to act like she is just yours, feel like she is just yours, make it plain to others that she is just yours — and still have another girl to the extent that you have Mimi. You just can't do it . . . Please try to see, and feel, very clearly and very honestly how you would feel and react if over the past six months Sue had another boy here whom she treated as you treat Mimi. . . . Jimmy, if you want "out" then you must figure the way to have "out", but don't break a girl's heart, don't hurt people. If you and Sue aren't right for each other then it shouldn't be. You will know these things. But don't keep her like she is tied up in a box with your name on it while you find out how you feel . . . If any guy had ever treated me that way! I just would never have taken it, I don't know any girl that would. It's completely unfair, all one-sided . . . Oh honey, I'm always on your side, but this time I don't understand your thinking . . . You are only 18, but if you must have more than one girl, then the one girl has got to be as free as you yourself are.

The thing was, I was infatuated with Mimi Tcheou and Sue and I were bickering as usual. I wrote back that I believe Sue did have freedom to date. She talked to me of Dick Bettinger, Roger Lehman, two very decent guys in her class. I didn't think I was requiring her to tell everyone she was attached to me. And I'm pretty sure I told my mother that, deep down, I wasn't sure which girl was the right one, though I was certainly agog over Mimi.

My mother needed to hear that in my own mind I was not entrapping my longtime high school girlfriend. Mom wrote right back: *"I have my 'facts straight' now — but how could they be straight until you told me? . . . It turns out there is more to it. Thank you for putting me straight." And then she wrote, ever on her oldest son's side: "Don't you know that I am just as happy as I can be because you found that wonderful Mimi?"*

Mimi was not looking forward to my going back to Pittsford and her going back to Manhattan. At the end of the year it was Mom who drove up to bring me home. I had asked her if we could drop Mimi off at the Rochester airport for her flight back to New York City. She agreed. Mimi sat between us in the front seat holding my hand the whole way.

After we saw her to her flight and she reached up for a kiss and lingering hug, I headed home with Mom. I knew she was going to say something. Listening to my mother was an inestimable treat. She was wise, considerate and thoughtful. Her soft voice always soothed, but she could also challenge her sons.

"Jimmy, you have to make up your mind. It's not fair to either girl, what you are doing," she said.

That's just about all she said. No long lecture, not who was the better girl for me, just, quite simply, I had to stop two-timing. I told her I knew she was right and I would figure it out. But I truly didn't know in my heart right then which girl I wanted.

Mimi had asked me to come and visit and she promised to write often. She did, lovely letters almost every day.

Mid-summer three high school friends, Charlie Hanner and Bill Bohn from the baseball team and Lefty Dalton, were driving to New York City and asked me to join them. We bought tickets to a Yankees game, to Sammy Davis Jr. in "Golden Boy" on Broadway and had an invitation to dinner at Mimi Tcheou's home, a small apartment in Chinatown. Her parents, Chinese immigrants, weren't crazy that their oldest daughter was dating someone who wasn't Chinese, but they served a delicious steak dinner and were incredibly hospitable.

There I was, my first time ever in Yankee Stadium with my college girlfriend sitting next to me and Mickey Mantle in the outfield. I thought, it doesn't get any better than this. It was an afternoon game and afterward there was a little time before the play. My friends went off into Manhattan. I took Mimi to our motel room. She was exceptionally amorous, wrapping her perfect little body around me and I loved being captured by her. But, we hadn't "done it" yet. We pulled back that day before the bliss exploded, leaving us both a little frustrated.

More so come September. Sue purposely failed her entrance exams to Skidmore College, where her parents wanted her to go. They reluctantly allowed her to head to Brockport State, the first college-bound Hastings who didn't go to an expensive private university. Now I had two girls on campus and they both knew it.

Choosing which girl wasn't the only dilemma starting my sophomore year. Money was always a concern. The summer job on the golf course was a big help, but it was clear I needed more. I went to Dean Welch to ask about campus work and he happened to have a vacancy for janitor at the student union, sweeping and mopping floors, and cleaning toilets. I took it — a one-night-a-week gig, late Saturday into Sunday morning. The messiest place was the third-floor billiard room, ash trays filled with butts, and wastebaskets full of junk food wrappers and empty paper coffee cups. Down the hall was a carpeted lounge with a big TV, couches and easy chairs. The student newspaper and student government offices were there. The second floor was deans' offices.

The janitor job put a little crimp in Saturday night carousing, but then the varsity soccer team's training rules forbade such activities anyway (not that everyone followed them). Every Saturday night at 11 p.m., sometimes midnight, I'd go clean the union, except for the first floor (the food service staff took care of the first floor.) I was glad of that. Between meals, the cafeteria is where we all hung out in plastic chairs at tables for four or pushed together if needs be. We chatted, debated, got to know each other in the din of jukebox music — Sam and Dave: "Hold On, I'm Comin'", The Four Tops: "Baby I Need Your Lovin'", the Rolling Stones: "I Can't Get No (Satisfaction)"; the Box Tops: "The Letter"; of course the Beatles belting out "Sgt. Pepper's Lonely Hearts Club Band" and more great new sounds, three songs for a quarter. Bob Champaigne would always play "Green Onions" by Booker T and the M.G.'s — and he taught us how to dance the green onion too.

They all stick in memory. Music is such a sweet salve. Even today, for no reason at all, John Fred and His Playboy Band pops into my head with "Judy in Disguise." It is a great semi-dissonant sound — "come to me tonight, come to me tonight" right down to the last, teasing line: "I guess I'll just take your glasses." Or Linda Ronstadt belting out "Different Drum" with the

Stone Poneys: "You and I travel to the beat of a different drum . . ."

I simply didn't want to be sweeping and mopping floors in that prized hangout and was glad the first floor wasn't part of my job. When I was sweeping upstairs Saturday nights, my mind would sometimes meander back to the day my father took me to his job at Friden in downtown Rochester and how he stopped on the stairs to talk to the janitor. It was such a generous gesture. I upgraded the position and told everyone I was now a "custodial engineer."

It was in the union that I met Mary Flanagan, who would marry Fred Harrington.

She was a friendly and pretty girl with brownish-red hair, freckles, a captivating smile, and an ear for good music. We would sit at a table with the jukebox playing, eating fries and drinking Coke. We'd talk about American poets; she could quote them, which simply amazed me. She even liked talking about the soccer games.

Mary was a good student who was also fully into the fun side of campus life. She got me into this Friday afternoon drinking club called WiTiFs — the F stood for Fridays, usually. It was unwind time, a few of the younger professors and a gaggle of students who cut out of Friday afternoon classes as fast as they could. With Mary it was easy. She made things fun and she didn't know it probably, but she challenged me to pay more attention to poetry — not just reciting it, but what it meant. We'd sometimes debate Poe or Wordsworth at WiTiFs until it felt like we were getting too serious. Bob Champaigne offered up political satire, but we never delved deeply into national issues. At most it was 20 people Friday afternoons, sometimes at Higgins downtown, and sometimes at the classier Roxbury Inn closer to campus. We'd run into each other and walk, or Mary would be there when I arrived. We developed a fine friendship, nothing more, but lasting. Though we live in different states, to this day we remain friends. She is my first-born daughter's godmother.

My new-found love of learning was invigorating to the extent that I switched out of teacher training into liberal arts with a major in American history. I found a class in American literature to be fascinating. We were reading Hemingway's "The Sun Also Rises." In high school I skipped Fitzgerald's "The Great Gatsby" by reading the Cliffs Notes. Not anymore.

I was astounded by the characters in Hemingway's novel. I was completely absorbed and loved to be prepared for class discussion.

One day Professor Curran asked the class, "OK, who can tell us what's wrong with Jake Barnes and his relationship with Lady Ashley?"

Everyone was silent, including me. He waited. I was about to offer that Lady Ashley seemed to stray some, when this beautiful redhead a few seats away blurted out, "He had his balls blown off in the war!"

I was shocked. I hadn't read that, but I kept my mouth shut as she and Mr. Curran exchanged views on the nature of love and relationships when something physically gets in the way. I felt stupid. I thought I had understood this great author. I loved the way he wrote, but how could I miss that? When class was over and the redhead (I can't remember her name) had walked out and no one else was there, I went up to Mr. Curran and said, "How could I have missed that? Where is it? Is it clear, explicit? Or is it implied?" I was very upset with myself. He took his copy of the book, fingered through a few pages and showed me two places: "Here Jim, on page 15," and he pointed at the passage:

She cuddled against me and I put my arm around her. She looked up to be kissed. She touched me with one hand and I put her hand away.

"Never mind."

"What's the matter? Are you sick?"

"Yes."

And then on pages 16-17:

" . . . we touched glasses.

"You're not a bad type," she said. "It's a shame you're sick. We got on well. What's the matter with you anyway?"

"I got hurt in the war," I said.

"Oh that dirty war."

"I don't believe I missed that!" I told my professor.

"It's OK, don't worry. But as we keep reading, now you know and it will help you judge these characters and their actions. You're doing fine," he told me.

I went back and re-read from the beginning and read over and over the passages where we learned of his war wound. So you think you're so smart,

I said to myself. Pay attention to what you are reading! In the end Professor Curran recommended me for honors English courses the next semester.

By then Sue's presence on campus trumped my time with Mimi. I awkwardly let her know that Sue was my girl. Was it hard? Yes. Even though we never consummated our relationship, I was still attracted to Mimi, but Sue and I went back to when she was 14 just turning 15. It was more than the force of habit. Sue was rooted deep inside me. Mimi responded by asking an old high school boyfriend to visit. He was a pre-med student and every time he visited, she let me know he had to stay in my dorm room, and one thing we didn't do was double-date.

Mimi was, in those years in the mid-1960s, the sexiest girl and, at the same time, one of the nicest people I had ever met. Near graduation, she gave me a fetching photo of herself and wrote on the back of it, "I will always remember you."

It is a cliché, but it is true that I think of her often. We've caught up with each other, off and on over the years, touchstones in a long life.

I turned 19 and found another part-time job, in the college library's magazine section. It was another eye-opener. My job was to put the magazines back on the display shelves where they belonged and generally keep the section neat and tidy. I never even considered there were so many magazines with so much knowledge at my fingertips. "Foreign Affairs," "The Wilson Quarterly," journals in chemistry, literary journals. I'd pick up a copy and find myself immersed in information I had never thought about. My GPA was 3.2, an A and all B's.

The honors English course included the Transcendentalists and we were assigned to read and critique Thoreau's "Walden." I was reading in the library one afternoon and simply lost myself in his prose:

This is a delicious evening, when the whole body is one sense, and imbibes delight through every pore. I go and come with a strange liberty in Nature, a part of herself. As I walk along the stony shore of the pond in my shirt-sleeves, though it is cool as well as cloudy and windy, and I see nothing special to attract me, all the elements are unusually congenial to me.

(I collected my books at the table and got up to leave without knowing it).

The bullfrogs trump to usher in the night, and the note of the whip-poor-will is borne on the rippling wind from over the water.

(I walked past the checkout desk without knowing it).

Sympathy with the fluttering alder and poplar leaves almost takes away my breath; yet, like the lake, my serenity is rippled but not ruffled. These small waves raised by the evening wind are as remote from storm as the smooth reflecting surface.

(I walked out the front door, down the steps and onto the sidewalk).

Though it is now dark, the wind still blows and roars in the wood, the waves still dash, and some creatures lull the rest with their notes. The repose is never complete . . .

I was standing in the middle of the street when a car's horn honked and brought me out of Walden Pond. It's true, I got up from where I was reading and out into the street still at Walden Pond with Thoreau's prose filling my mind, until that car honked at me.

Some of that book is pretty dry, but I got lost in it. I began to understand the power of good writing and of embracing ideas never considered before. I became studious and I was disappointed when I got less than A in any course. I started keeping a journal.

One night Bob Champaigne and I took a Greyhound bus into Rochester. For some reason I had my American literature text with me. On an impulse, I stood up in the aisle and read aloud Poe's "The Raven." The other passengers were initially puzzled, but when I finished they gave me a big round of applause. I passed my hat, and collected some extra beer money, which Bob and I surely needed.

I took an independent study course on Jacksonian democracy, which meant writing a 50-page thesis, consulting 47 works ranging from "The Diary of John Quincy Adams" to "A History of the American People" by Woodrow Wilson. I wrote that the beginnings of Jacksonian democracy "are a subject of controversy; some historians found its origins in the frontier wilderness, while others discovered those origins in the urban centers of the East. Some looked upon its aims as political while others saw it as economic, a social and even an intellectual movement." Professor F. K. Abbott supervised me and gave me an A. In fact, my GPA rose to 3.6, all A's and one B.

I challenged Tom Lawson, my roommate, a math major, to a contest. I was done with math (thank God), but I challenged him on who could get the higher grade on our next assignment, he in English and me in physics (for non-science majors), the closest to math that I had. I don't remember what I came up with, but Tom blew me away with a poetry assignment where he wrote: "What is peace of mind worth? See how easily the neatly piled leaves scatter."

"You wrote that?" I demanded, looking at the A on his paper.

"Yep."

"How did you think of that? How could a guy with his head full of numbers and formulas come up with that?"

"Dunno, just came to me."

"Wow, OK, you win."

He won free beers that night at our favorite bar, the Colonial Inn, just three or four blocks from campus. Draft beers were 10 cents. We could drink 10 beers for a dollar. And that night Lawson had more than his usual two.

At the end of January, 1966, my father was driving me back to campus after a visit home. It was snowing. Then it was snowing harder. Back then, forecasts weren't what they are now. We didn't know we were driving into the great blizzard of '66. He dropped me off at the dorm and headed back to Pittsford. After a few miles where he lost track of the road, he thought better of it, somehow turned around and got his car into the student union parking lot. He became my roommate for four days. The wind howled across the campus's flat open spaces. More than three feet of snow fell. Drifts were halfway up the buildings.

When it finally stopped snowing, but nothing was moving, Bob Champaigne and I trudged and crawled and managed to get across the athletic fields to the Physical Education building, where he knew there were some snowshoes. We found them and suddenly we were about the only mobile people on the campus. Some of the food service staff had stayed in the dining halls when the snow came and Bob and I began delivering sandwiches to hungry students stuck in their dorms. They called us lifesavers, but Bob and I were wholly enjoying walking on top of four feet of snow.

My father was tiring of card games, chess and listening to rock 'n' roll music he didn't really like. He suggested helping me with my janitorial duties. We walked from my dorm through the basement hallway to the student union and mopped and swept to our hearts' content. The next morning, the fourth of his stay, he was able to get to his car and drive home.

Junior year I gave up being a custodial engineer Saturday nights and working in the library because I became an RA, resident assistant. That gave me free room and board to be some kind of mentor/disciplinarian in a dorm. Except for my first three years on earth, it was the first time I had a room of my own. Sue also became an RA, not that she needed the money, it's that she wanted a room to herself, allowing me to climb in her window after dark.

We were in our own little world at Brockport in 1967, rarely aware of life outside campus. But in a long passage in my journal for March 12, 1967, I have a fleeting reference to "perhaps this is what President Johnson means when we discriminate against the poor in our draft laws." There we were, safe from the military draft as college students, but I wrote, "I am poor and I have paid my own way — it is not right to say draft laws discriminate against the poor." I concluded in a haughty and narrow-minded fashion that it was lack of opportunity or initiative, not poverty, that made the difference between being drafted and going to college. I don't recall any of us getting into national debates, no one on campus demonstrated against the Vietnam war; heck, virtually all the male students still had brush cuts. Just a year later Lyndon Johnson would announce he wasn't seeking re-election, he knew he couldn't win because of the war, but we at Brockport State preferred to look inward.

Except for a very few, like James Howard Kunstler, who arrived from Manhattan with a guitar, a harmonica and long, straight blonde hair nearly down to his shoulders. He would sit on a knoll in the middle of campus and sing Dylan songs. Nearly everyone referred to him as a hippie, weird. One day, I sat down on the knoll with him. We talked about Bob Dylan and we became friends, the jock and the hippie. Jim became the editor of the student literary magazine, his junior and my senior year. He published two of my poems. Later in life he wrote several financially unsuccessful novels, but finally in middle age hit it huge with his nonfiction tome "The Geography of Nowhere," and several sequels. All of them were harsh critiques of our big-box store, oil-guzzling culture. Kunstler is one of Brockport's most illustrious graduates.

Tom Lawson had been elected treasurer of the student government and he and some other guys urged me to run for president. Bob Champaigne was running for president of the senior class. We figured we'd get all the jocks to come out and vote, which they hardly ever did in student elections — a sure-fire win.

It worked. And I could rightly claim that in my college career I went from janitor to president. Bob and I and my whole ticket celebrated at the Roxbury, the classy bar in town with its waxed-to-a-sheen oak bar, hanging chandelier and flowered wallpaper. In the middle of the reverie a bottle of champagne was delivered, along with a telegram: "May 3, 1967. To President Jim Smith. We are the proudest people in town. Those who live at 25 North Main Street."

I wrote in my journal: "I won the election 604 to 272. Jim Smith — President Brockport Student Government. One big job. Good luck sir!!" And it was a paying job, essentially covering the cost of room and board for my senior year.

The campus newspaper, The Stylus, wasn't exactly ecstatic at my victory. We put together a whole ticket with a platform that included "Closer working relations with the Stylus including periodic checks as to how the paper can function most effectively." I didn't much like the editor and our proposal was truly a bald-faced attempt at controlling him.

Fat chance. The April 28, 1967, Stylus editorial endorsement read that, "The Progressive Expansion Party has an impressive slate of candidates (but) we feel that we can run this paper without the supervision of student government." It was my first lesson in a free press. We won the election but lost the support of the student newspaper.

The whole ticket won except for the pretty Peggy Klotz, whom we had drafted late when our original candidate for recording secretary dropped out. Peggy lost by only 37 votes. Howie Mabie, the ruggedly handsome co-captain of the soccer team, ran for student athletics coordinator; Ray Skinner, a tall, popular, wavy-haired rascal-on-campus for vice president; Gerry Bingeman, treasurer-elect behind Lawson (the treasurer position was a two-year gig); all won comfortably. The red-haired beauty Kathy Jackson trounced her opponent for corresponding secretary, while her boyfriend,

Mel Russo, won by just 11 votes for student activities director.

He got us into trouble first thing senior year in September 1967 by signing the raucous rock band Doug Clark and the Hot Nuts to a campus performance. Russo, Lawson and I were called into President Albert W. Brown's office, where he berated us for being "foolish and irresponsible." The band was famous on the college circuit then for their risqué song lyrics and jokes, and for performing in various states of undress. Their signature song was "Hot Nuts"; others were "My Ding-a-ling," "Big Jugs" and "The Bearded Clam."

Lawson was the most straight-laced kid I ever met. He was against bringing in the band and was refusing to pay for it, probably overstepping his authority. For an hour and a half Mel and I defended our choice and then Dean of Students Oliver Spaulding, amazingly, took our side. It was Lawson who solved the impasse. He suggested moving the band from campus to the popular College Inn dance hall downtown. Brown liked that. He liked people who could find solutions. What a great time at the Hot Nuts performance. I think Lawson decided not to go.

Our more impressive goal and platform plank was to get rid of women's hours. Men on campus could come and go as they pleased, but women in the dorms had to sign in by 10 p.m. weeknights, 11 p.m. Fridays and midnight Saturdays. This was not only unequal, but made for inconveniently early dates.

When we took office, we put it to a plebiscite. The college administration was tiring of in loco parentis, but wasn't crazy about the urgency of our drive, and insisted on parents' permission for any woman under 21. The Stylus covered the issue pretty well. Overwhelmingly, the student body voted to get rid of women's hours, except for freshmen women. The women's government actually argued that freshmen women (not men) "must earn" the right. At least their hours were moved to 12:30 a.m. week nights and 2:30 a.m. weekends.

I wrote in my journal March 21, 1968, "The thing passed."

I'd write not only my thoughts, however brief, in my journal, but I'd also put down quotations I came upon and admired, like Emerson's "If eyes were made for seeing, then beauty is its own excuse for being." Or Thoreau's

"Time is but the stream I go a fishing in . . . I see the sandy bottom and detect how shallow it is. Its thin current slides away but eternity remains." Or Pope's "A little learning is a dangerous thing; drink deep or taste not the Pierian Spring." I had to look up Pierian Spring. And Franklin's "Be ashamed to catch yourself idle." And Huck Finn: "The sky looks ever so deep when you lay down on your back in the moonshine; I never knowed it before." I figured Franklin would forgive such idleness. And I wrote this down: "One basic liberty. Freedom of press — the uncontrolled and uncensored exchange in print of ideas, information, arguments and accusations — is in many ways the essential political liberty. The effective conduct of free government is dependent upon the existence of a free press; the fortunes of each seem always to rise and fall together." Cornell historian Clinton Rossiter wrote it in his book, "The First American Revolution."

The fortunes of a free government depending on a free press literally came true for me as president of the student government. A new editor took over at The Stylus. She was only a sophomore. I'll call her Sherry. I asked her if I could write a column as president and she agreed — the free press giving the freely elected government a little lift. Now I could inform everyone what we were trying to accomplish and I could put it in my own words.

Sue and I were struggling. We were bickering again, fighting, not getting along. I remember saying to her, exasperated, "Sue, I'm carrying a full load of classes. I'm the starting left wing on the varsity soccer team. I'm running the student government. C'mon, give me a break!" She wore my pin, which was the thing in college then before you got engaged. We decided she'd take it off. We'd take a break. We were free to date others. It was in early October, midway in the soccer season. I sadly but honestly felt I'd dropped a big burden. And I hoped she would be OK. She sure didn't seem happy with me and maybe I was just too damn busy.

I ran into Sherry in a bar one night. I was one of the few soccer players who didn't drink in season. I had a Coke. We talked and I told her Sue and I had broken up. She was smart, informed and had a friendly, quick wit. I walked her to her dorm. She was tall, 5' 6" I thought, different than walking with the 5' 2" Sue. Sherry had short, dark, wavy hair, a pretty face and easy smile.

We had our first date, editor and president. I talked about how much younger she was and that we might be playing with fire. We ended up in the back seat of Lawson's car self-consciously fumbling around when I came upon a safety pin in her bra strap. I had heard about the old trick to stop entry but had never happened upon it. I sat up and said, "Boy, you are young, aren't you!"

She pulled me down and smothered me in kisses.

Then it was Sherry coming to varsity soccer games and not Sue. In one game I jumped high for the ball intending to execute a scissors kick, but came down wrong, hitting my head on the ground. The next thing I knew, I was running around but didn't know why. I didn't know where I was. I couldn't remember my name. Before I panicked, I slowed down and brought the word "soccer" to my thoughts. Then "Brockport," but I had no idea who we were playing. I ran to the bench, somehow remembered my coach's name and cried, "Mr. Parker, take me out!"

Assistant coach Joe Drum laid me down on the ground and had me count fingers. He asked me my name, he asked me the score — "What score?" I said.

They got me to the college infirmary, gave me something and I fell asleep. When I woke up, sitting in a chair right next to my bed was Sherry. I knew her right away. I said "What am I doing here?"

I probably had a mild concussion, but I seemed fine. And it felt ever so good that she was there waiting for me.

Pretty soon Sherry and I were everywhere together. We went to all the dances and she showed me how to dance — "bend your knees, like this," she said; "look, like this," and I saw her dip to the rhythm of Sam and Dave's "Hold On I'm Comin'." I didn't know what a lousy, stiff-legged dancer I had been. You had to bend your knees to the beat, dummy! Sherry and I danced and danced and danced. I loved dancing with her. She was an incredible dancer. Mimi Tcheou was ever so smooth on the dance floor, but she couldn't show me how, the way Sherry so easily and naturally did.

This was only the second time I drifted away from Sue since I met her at her 15th birthday party. When I was with Mimi, Sue was still back in high school, and yet there was at least a subliminal nagging in my cranium,

Catholic guilt if you will, about which girl was for me. Sue wore Golden Autumn perfume, an earthy, musky presence that somehow helped anchor her high-energy intensity. Mimi used Wind Song. It seemed to cradle us on a soft white cloud of intimacy. To this day it stays on my mind; if a woman walks by with a Wind Song scent, it reels me right back to my freshman heartthrob. If Sherry wore perfume, I never noticed. She was an open book, a genuine, trusting, accepting, hold-me-babe girl who simply said, "Here I am." Oh, she had boundaries, and maybe that was part of why I couldn't resist.

In a winter storm, the power went out campus-wide. Somehow the student newspaper editor and the student government president were in the same car with Dean of Students Spaulding and college President Brown. We were checking on the dorms and went to a facilities plant to see when the power could get back up. Brown got the word out that if you could find accommodations with friends off campus, to do so. So Sherry came with me to a room I shared in a house with Lawson a couple blocks off campus. And she slept with me. Lawson was quite uncomfortable, glaring at me from his bed across the room. But I paid him no mind and Sherry wasn't budging. She pulled the blankets over our heads and wrapped her arms around me. When we awoke, my girl and I still had all our clothes on. She drew the lines.

Sue was dating a soccer teammate; he had even asked me permission. I assured him we had broken up and I actually felt relieved that she was with him. He'd have his hands full, I thought and I smiled to myself.

The first time I heard from home about my new girlfriend, my mother was expressing some trepidation. She must have thought, oh no, here we go again. First Mimi and now Sherry. Her letter arrived on Dec. 12, my 21st birthday. *"I hope it's a good, happy day. It's always happy for me, it's the day I got you."*

But she was sad this day. *"Sue and I talk now and then and I'm sorry she is so unhappy . . . she surely misses you terribly."*

I had developed serious feelings for my editor, and she for me. She told me she loved me; that she was in love with me. Being Jewish shouldn't matter, right? she asked. I absolutely agreed. In fact, I was surprised when she told me she was Jewish. I made it clear that her religion didn't matter at all to me. I must have told her I was Catholic, but it was clear different religious beliefs were not getting in the way of our relationship. They were simply irrelevant. I took her home to meet my parents and we went to my brother Steve's varsity basketball game in the same gym where I used to play. He was a dominating high school basketball star.

On Jan. 12, 1968, my mother was ready to show support, even though I knew she had doubts. In another of her remarkably supportive letters, she wrote, *"Do you have it in your head that I (and others here at home) are unhappy with you because you broke up with Sue? . . . First of all, you have nothing at all to feel guilty about. If it wasn't right, it wasn't. And thank God you had the courage to make things right. If they aren't right yet, or you aren't sure they are, please just let time go by and things will straighten out as they should . . . don't you know that your feelings, your convictions, your future are more important to us than anything?"*

"Let time go by." I was so comforted by that, though sometimes I wanted time to stand still. I wanted Sherry and me to know each other more deeply. I wanted guilt over jilting Sue to flow out of my thoughts.

It became clear to me that Sherry's father was as protective of his daughter as my mother was of me. They lived near the north shore of Long Island. She talked about her father all the time. She idolized him. I think, though, he was more worried about religious differences than we were. One day I came across the two of them in the student union, arguing. He had driven up all the way from Long Island. He was worried. They hadn't seen me coming up the stairs and I knew it was her father because she was saying, "But Dad, I love him."

They were face to face, going at it. I walked quickly by and I don't think she noticed me. I don't think I brought it up. I don't think I told her about my mother's advice. I wanted us to work based on us, on how we felt, not on how our parents felt. But catching her by chance with her dad, it certainly helped me know how serious she was about me. She started talking about our future. I had applied to a couple of graduate schools. She told me she was going with me. "I'll quit school and get a job and support us, until you finish," she said, and meant it. How could I let her jeopardize her own education? I didn't think I could let her do that. I knew I should be thinking about my future, but mostly I kept saying to myself, I just didn't want college to end. But here I was in my last semester.

I truly enjoyed, loved being with Sherry. I loved her. Some nights in bed

I'd let my mind wrestle with the difference between "love" and "in love." How odd, I thought — we never fought. Conversation was easy both ways. I listened with interest at what she had to say and she reciprocated. We had one flag of warning. She came up with the phrase "bailing out." She asked me to let her know if "bailing out" crept into my feelings, my thoughts. Would we? Would one of us bail out first? But it was a safety valve in the background. We were simply having too much fun and it felt so good being with her.

Months into our relationship one evening in the student government office we were making out on the couch when, for the first time, things really heated up physically. For the first time, pieces of clothing were about to come off when Lawson opened the door and walked in. We jumped up, smiled at him and walked out a tad disheveled and red-faced. It was as if we were magnetized in our own force field, but even then being in love did not mean, for Sherry, going all the way. In the very beginning, probably that first date in the backseat of Lawson's car, she told me she was a virgin and she's not ready to give that up yet. I thought that was something special and I wasn't going to force the issue. I was simply engrossed in everything about her. I liked everything about her.

Gradually, though inevitably I suppose, my old guilt began to creep back in again. Sue had dropped poundage that she characteristically gained when she was stressed. Her parents had bought her a new lime green Mustang. She was the hottest babe on campus, (with the possible exception of Janet Pearl, a gorgeous physical education major). Sue roared by me one March afternoon, stopped, backed up and said, "Let's go for a ride."

She drove all over. We talked. She said she wasn't enjoying my teammate one bit.

"Are you really in love with Sherry?" she asked.

I told her I better get out, could she drop me off. I was panicking. Here I go again, which girl is it? I skipped my afternoon classes. I walked and walked. I missed dinner. I walked some more. It was dark. Then it was near midnight and I was in the student government office. I couldn't move. I literally was unable move. I sat there and thought about Sherry and thought about Sue. I thought about jumping out the window, but I couldn't move. I thought about calling my mother, but I couldn't raise my arm. I was frozen. I stared at the phone book. It was as if I could hear time ticking while I was unmovable. I stared and stared and, gradually, like binoculars coming into focus, an idea was forming in my mind. I finally was able to pick up the book and turn the pages to "S," looking for Spaulding, Oliver Spaulding, dean of students. He was a great guy. He and I worked on all kinds of things together that senior year of 1967-68. I found his home number. I dialed the phone sometime after midnight.

A sleepy voice answered.

"Mr. Spaulding," I whispered, "I, I."

"Jim," he said immediately. "Is that you?"

"Yes."

"Where are you?"

I told him and he said, "Don't move, I'll be right there."

I didn't move. And soon he was there. We went down a flight of stairs to his office. I was a tad incoherent, "Sue, Sherry…"

He listened. He said supportive things. He was terrific. He had saved me from some frightening zone I had never been in before. And then he said something he probably shouldn't have, or maybe he did it on purpose because he knew it had force. He was truly trying to bring me out of whatever myopia I was in.

"It's not my choice; it's yours, Jim, but I think it's probably Sherry," he said.

Right at that exact moment, upon hearing that, I knew it wasn't. It wasn't Sherry. It was Sue. I don't know why I knew it, nor why I knew it right then. Oliver Spaulding was a mentor to me. His advice meant something to me. I almost wanted to thank him for giving me clarity when I had been in a deep fog that night. But I couldn't find the words. Nor could I articulate why I was going back to Sue. I couldn't grasp what alchemy bubbled up to separate me from a happy, understanding dark-haired girl I loved being with to the pretty blonde who could be such a project. Maybe we just had too much history, going back to 1962. When you are just 21, six years is a long time, nearly a third of your life. I managed to thank Dean Spaulding for coming out so late. He made sure I could walk, that I was OK, and then he went home. I walked the two blocks to my house.

I didn't tell anyone I had met with him. The next night I ran into Sue and got in her Mustang. She didn't say much. She just drove fast from campus, out of town, down Route 101 to a cheap motel. We stayed the night. She felt so familiar. She never went all the way with anyone else but me.

Sherry and I had a tearful good-bye. I think I've blocked out that moment. I know I said "bailing out." Her many friends called me a two-timer and worse, and I felt they were good friends to her. I felt awful, horrible, for breaking up with such a good woman. I was filled with guilt, but I had made my choice.

The campus Newman Center priest, whom I had known for four years, told me, "You better get married quick."

Just before graduation I received a card from Sherry. She wrote: "Jim, What can I say, Babes? Just tons and tons of good luck always — Love, me." What a class act.

I had given Sue a small diamond ring. I told my parents we were getting married. In fact we were getting married one week after graduation, two months away. I was 21. Sue was 20. Her parents objected to the rush. But we got married June 15, 1968, a week after I graduated. Sue, a beautiful bride, still had one semester to go in the fall before she could graduate. We moved into a house on the farm in Pittsford where I had worked summers and where Sue used to bring cold lemonade when I was baling hay. I worked on the farm that summer. We had been practicing birth control, but to our surprise, Sue got pregnant. We went back to Brockport where she finished up, including a required physical education course, playing tennis as her pregnancy showed more and more.

One night I was on campus and went past a dining hall where there was a dance. I looked in and saw Sherry dancing with a guy. Oh how she could dance. I paused, then kept walking.

The following spring my first daughter, Barbara Ann Smith, would be born.

THE END

Acknowledgments

This book is my writing and my responsibility, but I am indebted to several people, some who know Pittsford, some who know writing. My editor, Glenn Richter, always makes a story better. Jacky Smith, Steve Smith and Susan Hastings Lunt read the full, early manuscript and offered thoughtful advice. Susan Schadt provided terrific book design. Bill Bruce, Bob Champaigne, Barbara Ann Davis, Paula Derrow, Dan Dowling, Fred Harrington, Janie Dowling Kincaid, Dan Klau, Tom Lawson, Brooke Morse, Jim Palmer, Betsy and Roger Powers, Stephanie Smith, Andy Smith and Bill Smith, were especially helpful. Reid MacCluggage and Carol Giacomo, great scribes, offered the essential encouragement to a man at work. I am deeply indebted to Ruth Crocker at Elm Grove Press for her wisdom and encouragement and for publishing this book. You can't write about Pittsford without a shout out to Paul Spiegel, the longtime Town Supervisor and author of excellent volumes on the town's history. Also insightful and helpful was "Reflections on Big Spring, A History of Pittsford, NY and the Genesee River Valley" by David McNellis.

CPSIA information can be obtained
at www.ICGtesting.com
Printed in the USA
JSHW021917261120
9806JS00005B/120

9 781940 863054